Beverley Sutherland Smith's

ORIENTAL
COOKBOOK

Healthy, easy recipes from Asia

Beverley Sutherland Smith's

ORIENTAL COOKBOOK

Healthy, easy recipes from Asia

The Five Mile Press

The Five Mile Press
P.O. Box 327
Poole Dorset BH15 2RG United Kingdom

First published 1990

Design by Derrick Stone
Photography by Mannix

Typeset by Post Typesetters, Brisbane
Printed in Singapore by Kyodo Printing Co. Ltd.

Cataloguing-in-Publication data

Sutherland Smith, Beverley.
   Beverley Sutherland Smith's oriental cookbook.

   Includes index
   ISBN 0 86788 294 8

   1. Cookery, Oriental. I. Title. II. Title : Oriental cookbook.

641.593

ACKNOWLEDGEMENTS

The author and Publishers wish to
express their gratitude to
the Wing Wah Trading Co.
for the loan of the Oriental
china and pottery used in the
photographs in this book.

COVER PHOTOGRAPH
Rich Beef Soup with Noodles, p.42,
and nuoc mam, p.43.

CONTENTS

INTRODUCTION

As a child I was taken out to dinner with my family only on special occasions. For years, I naively believed that dining out meant eating chop suey, sweet and sour pork and fried rice in a restaurant with Laminex tables and red lanterns. The local Cantonese restaurant, with its particular style of cooking, was all most of us knew about eating out — or about Asian food — in those days.

It wasn't until many years later, after such a variety of Asian restaurants became established throughout Australia, and after travelling to Asia myself, that the whole spectrum and wonder of Oriental cooking was unfolded to me. I then realised that the structure and history of each country was reflected in its cuisine.

I once read that nobody can truly understand and cook the food of a country unless they have spent most of their lives there. Perhaps this is so, but even if true understanding is not attainable, the enjoyment and adventure of cooking foods from other countries is open to us all.

In this book a small range of dishes has been selected from several Asian countries, each dish chosen because it is light and healthy and, while still retaining its traditional style, can be cooked with ease in the average Western kitchen. People in Asian countries eat less fat, sugar and salt than we do. Emphasis is placed on health and well-being. Less meat is consumed, more fish, rice and vegetables being eaten instead. And even the simplest dish is prepared with great care and attention to detail, following rituals set by generations of cooks.

All dishes included are tasty and healthy. Most are easy to cook and can be put together in a multi-course meal or eaten separately. Where possible, I have tried to indicate how many serves each dish will make. But I will have to leave the final judgement up to your common sense because the number of serves will vary according to whether you are serving the dish as a main dish or side dish.

Remember, there's no reason why you can't do some mixing and matching of your own. For example, don't feel restricted by the conventions of any one country. You could serve a Vietnamese soup before a Western-style main course, or accompany a steak with a couple of Asian salads or a stir-fry. These dishes can be as flexible as you like, as long as the same rules of balancing tastes, cooking techniques and textures are followed as those applying to the composition of any dinner.

Ingredients are easy to obtain, thanks to all the migrants who have created the demand for them. These dishes are ideal for family cooking, but can be grand enough for entertaining. Above all, they suit modern lifestyles and the demand for fresher, lighter menus. So enjoy.

COOKING RICE

Rice is a major part of everyday life in most Asian countries, the huge family rice cooker and bowls of rice always present on the table. According to some of my reference books, the average Chinese consumes 500 grams (or a pound) of rice each day. It is the mainstay of the Asian diet; with a bowl of rice a smaller amount of meat or vegetables can be served.

Huge varieties of rice are grown: long grain, short grain, round or flat rice, even coloured rice. It is sensible to choose the style you like best and, as the Asians use so many different varieties, you can still feel your choice is 'authentic'.

In all Asian methods of cooking rice, the first step is always to 'wash it well'. This doesn't mean just a rinse but a real wash in lots of water. It is a ritual which signals the beginning of the meal preparation. As most rice in Western countries is not coated with cornflour, glucose or talcum powder — as it can be in Asia — this is not so vital, but I do find that the rice grain is less starchy and has a lighter taste, if well rinsed.

Put the rice in a bowl, cover with water and move it around with your hands; the water will become cloudy in about 10 seconds. Drain and repeat, returning the rice to the bowl and covering again with water. Each time drain well, and stir with your hands, but more gently as the water comes clear because the rice can begin to break as it softens. (Just rinsing briefly under the tap does nothing, so either give it the proper 3 minutes' rinsing in water or don't bother at all.) Once you have done this, the wet rice can be left aside until ready to cook.

I have included several methods of cooking rice — choose whichever you feel happiest with — and of course remember that rice can be reheated, either in a steamer or a bowl over water. Microwave heating is also most successful. None of these recipes, however, should be used for instant rice.

THE ABSORPTION METHOD OF COOKING RICE

This particular method should result in rice grains that are well defined, and for this I prefer to use long grain rice. It is best to use a pot that is deep rather than shallow so the water does not evaporate so quickly.

LONG GRAIN RICE

The quantity below makes enough rice to accompany a meal for six.

2 cups medium–long grain rice	*3 cups (24 fl oz) cold water*

Rinse the rice as described in the introduction of this chapter, and put into your saucepan. Add the water and bring to the boil. After it has boiled for about half a minute cover the pan with a tight-fitting lid.

Turn the heat down very low and let cook — it should be bubbling very slightly inside. Don't lift the lid; listen if not sure. Let the rice cook for 15 minutes, then remove from the heat but still don't open the pan.

Leave it sit for another 20 minutes. During this time the rice will absorb the steam, becoming tender and plump.

Gently fluff with a fork, lifting the grains up from the base so they are separated. You can leave the rice in the saucepan; it will keep warm for about another 15 minutes without spoiling. (If you need to keep it any longer it is best to let cool and then reheat.)

SHORT GRAIN RICE

2 cups short grain rice	*2½ cups water*

Follow the same method as for long grain rice. You need less water with short grain rice, but it is exactly the same technique.

CHINESE BOILED RICE

This easy Chinese method of cooking rice is supposedly 'fail-safe'.

2 cups long grain rice	*water*
salt	

Put the rice into a basin, cover generously with cold water, and stir well with your hands. Drain, return to the basin and repeat this about 3 times, or until the water is clear.

Transfer the rice to a saucepan and add cold water to come about

25cm (1 in) above the level of the rice. Add salt, and bring to boil. Reduce the heat and cook the rice with the lid slightly tilted (to let out some steam) until there is no water left above the rice.

Put the lid on firmly and cook over lowest heat for 20 minutes. Remove from the heat, and let it steam in the pan for 5 minutes. Then remove the lid and, using a fork, fluff up the rice.

Serves 6

BOILED RICE

This method of cooking rice is not used in Asian countries but I have included it because some people find it is the easiest method of all. The rice can be either served immediately or else can be reheated by placing it in a shallow bowl in a steamer until very hot.

1½ cups rice	*2 tsp salt*
10 cups water	

Rinse the rice under running water. There's no need to wash it quite as well as for the other methods of cooking, because the rice is cooked in so much water. Bring the water to the boil in a large saucepan, and add salt. When bubbling slowly sprinkle in the rice through your fingers, so the water remains on the boil.

Stir once to move the grains from the base of the pot, and cook uncovered, keeping the water constantly boiling. The timing will vary according to the rice.

Basmati takes about 8–10 minutes, and long grain, about 12–13 minutes. Always test by taking out a little rice with a spoon and tasting. It should be soft and yet a little resistant to your teeth, but should not have a hard centre. Drain in a sieve, and fluff lightly with a fork.

THAILAND

Thai cooking has become the flavour of the year, a cuisine which displays a skilful balance between sweet and sour, herbs, spices and salt; the five often being included in the one dish. Essentially, Thai food is simple, stir-fry cooking being the dominant method. The main ingredients are vegetables with rice, fish and spices. Meat is served only in small quantities. There is little fat, although I found the most popular dishes on most menus tend to feature coconut cream or milk which is high in fat, so these have been omitted. Lots of chili, garlic, lemon grass, shallots and onions, coriander, basil and shrimp paste or soy sauce are used.

Everything is beautifully sliced, designed to be bite-sized, so preparation is important. Cooking is fast, with lots of fresh, crunchy ingredients. Great skill is shown in cutting and carving vegetables and fruits and in the delicate decoration of platters taken to the table. Exotic displays of flowers are traditionally placed on the table.

The climate is so hot that much of their dining is casual and outdoors. Food does not have to be hot but is allowed to become tepid. In a Thai meal, dishes are not served in any particular order. Often, they are all placed on the table at once, with some tasty little side dishes adding highlights. If you prefer, you can serve them more traditionally: a salad dish and soup followed by a bowl of rice with a single main course.

Fresh limes are commonly used in Thai cooking, but lemons have been substituted in some of these dishes, because they are more readily available here.

PRAWN SOUP

This is the best-known of all the Thai soups. Made with raw prawns and seasoned with lime leaves and aromatic lemon grass, it is liberally spiked with chili.

It is hot, sour and clear, and is eaten throughout the meal in Thailand. Usually served in a charcoal-heated steamboat, the pink prawns are fished out and eaten first, while the stock reduces, becoming more fragrant and intense as the meal progresses.

There are many different versions of this soup. This is a home-style one. Note that you must buy prawns with shells on to get the flavour for the base of the soup otherwise, it will be an insipid copy of the real thing.

500g (1 lb) prawns (jumbo shrimp)	*4 cups (32 fl oz) chicken stock*
in the shell,	*1 chili, seeds removed and sliced*
1 tbsp oil	*1 tbsp fish sauce*
2 stalks lemon grass, top end	*2 tbsp lemon juice*
removed and inside part chopped	*2 tsp sugar*
fine	*fresh coriander leaves*
6 strips lime or lemon rind	*a few extra slivers of chili*

Shell the prawns, removing but retaining the heads and leaving on the little tail end.

Heat the oil in a large saucepan, add the heads and cook over high heat until they have changed colour. Crush the lemon grass a little with a pestle and mortar or the end of a rolling pin. Add with lemon rind and stock, and simmer very gently for about 20 minutes, skimming the top of any scum.

Add the chili, fish sauce, lemon juice and sugar; put a lid on the pan. Remove from the heat and let stand for about 5 minutes. Then pour this through a very fine sieve, pushing down gently to get all the juices from the heads.

Remove the dark vein from the prawns. When ready to serve, heat the stock. Add the prawns and cook gently for about 2 minutes. Remove from the heat, let stand about a minute or, if large prawns, for 2 or 3 minutes.

Add the coriander and a few fresh slivers of chili, if you want to increase the heat. Taste and adjust the seasonings of salt and lemon.

Once the prawns have been added the soup shouldn't be reheated or they will toughen so do this part of the dish only at dinnertime.

Serves 6

MUSHROOM AND CELERY SALAD

Refreshing with flavours of mint and lemon, this could be a side dish at a multi-course meal, an accompaniment for a Western-style meal, or could be served with seafood as a first course.

250 g (8 oz) mushrooms, cut into halves if small, quarters if large	1 tbsp fish sauce
1 cup thinly-sliced celery	1 tsp sugar
2 tbsp finely-chopped spring onion	½ red chili, seeded and finely chopped
2 tbsp lemon juice	1/3 cup mint leaves, finely shredded

Bring a medium-sized pan of water to the boil. Add mushrooms and let stand in the water for 1 minute. Drain.

If the celery is not crisp put into ice-water for 1 hour. Drain.

Mix mushrooms, celery and spring onions.

Mix all remaining ingredients in a bowl to make a dressing, then add to the mushroom mixture. Toss gently and stand for about 30 minutes before serving.

Serves 4 (as an accompaniment)

RED CURRY PASTE

Although it can be bought in Asian shops, this home-made curry paste is more aromatic, and keeps well for about a month. It makes about a third of a cup, and is quite easy to make if you have a blender. Otherwise, you'll need a pestle and mortar, and plenty of patience. Work the dry ingredients first in the mortar, then add the moist ones to make a paste.

20 dried chilies (minus seeds) or
 1½ tbsp cayenne pepper
5 shallots, finely chopped
1 tsp ground caraway seeds
1½ tbsp Laos powder
1 tsp salt
grated rind 2 lemons or 2 limes
1 stalk lemon grass, tough top
 removed and inside stalk finely
 chopped

1 tsp ground black pepper
2 tbsp whole coriander seeds
3 tbsp coriander roots, finely
 chopped
2 tbsp garlic, finely chopped
2 tsp shrimp paste
6 tbsp peanut oil

Put the chilies with shallots, caraway seeds, laos powder, salt, lemon rind, lemon grass, pepper, coriander seeds and roots, garlic and shrimp paste into a blender, and add half the oil. Turn on the blender and add the lemon rind, lemon grass, pepper, coriander seeds and roots, remainder of the oil, processing until you have a smooth paste.

FISH IN A RED SAUCE

The red sauce is tomato-based and except for the little touch of hot chili, this could be a dish from almost any country. Fish becomes beautifully moist and flavoursome cooked this way, between tomato layers. The tomato base can be made up to a day beforehand, making it a very easy dish. I find any filleted fish is suitable, except for very finely-textured ones. These are a little too fragile, and will break easily when removed from the sauce.

4 large fillets of fish, or 8 small fillets	1 tbsp white wine vinegar
1 tbsp oil	3 tsp sugar
2 medium-sized onions, finely diced	salt and pepper to taste
1 chili, seeded and chopped	chopped coriander, parsley or a
750 g (1½ lb) ripe tomatoes, peeled	little basil

Heat the oil in a saucepan, add the onion and cook gently until slightly softened. Put a lid on the pan and cook another 5 minutes until very tender. Add the chili, fry a minute.

Chop the tomatoes into rough pieces, add with vinegar, sugar and season. Cook until the sauce is moderately thick.

Tip half the sauce into a frying pan so it forms a thin layer on the base. Arrange fish on this, and spoon remaining sauce over the top. Bring gently to the boil and cover the pan. Turn the heat down very low and cook for about 5 minutes before turning off the heat. Let the fish sit in the sauce, and it will continue cooking in the warmth of the pan, remaining very moist.

The timing will depend greatly on thickness of the fish, but leave for about for 5 minutes, then check. If not cooked, you can always heat again for a couple of minutes.

Carefully remove the fish fillets to serving plates with a spatula or egg slice. Scatter coriander, parsley or basil over the top and serve.

There will be plenty of sauce, so accompany this with some rice alongside. Although not served this way in Thailand, I like some very fine noodles as an alternative to rice.

Serves 4

SAUTEED MIXED GREENS AND CHICKEN

A quick, easy and nourishing dinner. Obviously the range of greens used in Thailand is different from those available in cooler areas. I use spinach and lettuce and, if I can get baby ones, a tiny handful of beetroot tops. This dish only takes about 15 minutes of preparation, and a few minutes to cook.

2 tbsp oil	*½ bunch washed spinach, with*
4 cloves finely chopped garlic	*tough stalks removed*
250 g (8 oz) boned chicken breast,	*a small handful beetroot leaves*
finely diced	*1 tbsp fish sauce*
2 cups finely-shredded lettuce	*plenty of black pepper*

Heat the oil and add garlic. Fry for a few seconds, or until aromatic. Add the chicken and toss until it has changed colour. Remove.

Leave any oil or liquid in the pan and add the lettuce. Cook a couple of minutes, then add spinach and beetroot tops. Toss until the vegetables have just softened.

Mix the chicken back into the dish, seasoning with fish sauce and pepper. Serve immediately.

Serves 4

CHICKEN AND BASIL

In this original Thai dish, the basil is cooked in two ways: some is added to the chicken pieces, while the rest is fried in a little oil to make crispy green pieces, rather like fried parsley. As this book doesn't use much fried food, I have omitted the crispy basil — which I must admit is a perfect topping — just adding the extra basil as a fresh herb on top, instead. Different, but none the less delicious. A very quickly-cooked main course to serve with rice.

2 tbsp oil

3 cloves garlic, crushed or finely chopped

1 chili, finely chopped (minus seeds)

2 tsp grated fresh ginger

500 g (1 lb) raw chicken breast, boned and skinned and cut into fine strips

^{1}/$_3$ cup basil leaves

1 tbsp fish sauce

2 tsp sugar

2 tbsp water

an additional ¼ cup basil leaves, cut into fine shreds

Heat the oil, add garlic, chili and ginger and cook gently for a minute, or until aromatic.

Turn up the heat under the pan to high and add the chicken. Cook, tossing until it has changed colour. Add basil, then turn the heat low and cover the pan. Cook for about 2 minutes.

Add the fish sauce, sugar, and water, and cook for another minute. The chicken should be tender, with just a little sauce around.

Scatter on remaining basil, stir and serve immediately.

Serves 4

VEGETABLE AND PORK CURRY

Almost all Thai curries have one thing in common: they use generous amounts of rich coconut milk, which is delicious but high in fat. This homely dish is one of the few curries without coconut milk. It is a lighter curry than usual, and comes originally from Thai villages where there is not much time to prepare dinner. Quickly-cooked food is mostly served at night, after the day's work on the farm. The distinctive red curry paste can be bought ready-made. However, you can prepare this yourself, if you wish (see page 13). As the pork is not cooked for long, use a tender cut, such as fillet.

3 Chinese dried mushrooms

1 tbsp oil

1 tbsp red curry paste

375 g (12 oz) lean pork, cut into thin slices about 4 cm (1½ in.) square

1 stalk lemon grass, tough end removed and centre finely chopped

1 tbsp fish sauce

125 g (4 oz) cabbage, very finely shredded or cut into tiny squares

2 medium-sized carrots, cut into halves and then thin strips

90 g (3 oz) green beans, but into 5 cm (2 in.) pieces

1 chili, seeded and flesh finely diced

2 tbsp water

1 tsp sugar

about a dozen mint leaves, cut into thin shreds

Cover the mushrooms with hot water, and soak for about 20 minutes. Remove the tough stalk, and chop the mushroom in fine slices.

Heat the oil, add the curry paste and fry a few minutes, stirring.

Add the pork, and cook over medium heat until it has changed colour. Then mix in all the vegetables with the lemon grass and chili pieces, and stir-fry for about 5 minutes. Add the water, and sugar, and fry a few minutes longer. The pork should be tender at the same time as the vegetables. Just before serving, stir in the mint.   Serves 4

MEAT PATTIES

A Thai version of hamburgers, these are tasty and can be served with side-salads, rice or on toast or a bun, if you like hamburgers. (There's no reason why you can't adapt these patties in this way.)

---

250 g (8 oz) finely-minced lean
    beef
250 g (8 oz) finely-minced lean
    pork

1 tbsp fish sauce
1 tsp ground black pepper
1 tbsp cold water
1 egg white

TO BE GROUND

3 cloves garlic, finely chopped or
    crushed
1 tbsp coriander root chopped,

3 spring onions, thinly sliced
¼ cup coriander leaves (Chinese
    parsley)

Mix everything together; hands are best of all for this. When it binds and is all nicely blended, form into eight round patties. If sticky, wet your hands to form the rounds. These patties can be refrigerated, covered, for about 8 hours.

Cook either in a non-stick pan or use just a little oil, turning them over when brown on the first side. Cook through but keep moist in the centre.

Drain on some kitchen paper and serve immediately — although they are also very nice as a cold picnic dish.

Serves 4

GRILLED BEEF SALAD

Unlike our green salads, Thai salads are often made with meat. They have lovely light flavours, and are composed decoratively on the plate, usually a flat one, so the arrangement is more effective. A spicy dressing of some sort is poured over the top, and it is then decorated and garnished with perhaps mint and basil, a topping of peanuts and often flower petals.

Ideally, Thai salads are served at room temperature, rather than chilled.

---

1 small chili, sliced (minus seeds)

2 tsp lemon grass

½ tsp salt

500 g (1 lb) lean grilling quality beef

250 g (8 oz) fine noodles such as
   vermicelli

2 tbsp chopped basil

2 tbsp mint leaves, shredded

$^1/_3$ cup finely-chopped roasted
   peanuts

Put the chili, lemon grass and salt into a bowl and pound with the flat end of a rolling pin or use a pestle and mortar.

Cut the beef into thin slices, and scatter the chili mixture over the beef, turning so the pieces are lightly coated. Leave to marinate for an hour.

Spread the beef pieces out on a flat grilling (broiling) tray and put under a pre-heated griller until brown on one side. Turn over and cook just 30 seconds on the second side or until they have just changed colour. Be careful not to overcook.

Remove and cut the slices of beef into thin shreds when cool. Cook the noodles in a pot of boiling water until just tender. Drain. Put onto a plate. Top with beef.

SAUCE

3 tbsp white vinegar	1 small chili, finely chopped
3 tbsp sugar	(minus seeds)
½ tsp salt	2 tbsp finely-grated carrot
3 tbsp water	2 tbsp finely grated turnip.

Heat the vinegar, sugar, salt and water. Pound the chili and add to the water, with carrot and turnip. Bring to the boil. Remove and cool.

Spoon over the noodles and beef. Sprinkle the top with basil and mint, and scatter nuts on last.

Note: If you wish to prepare this beforehand, cook the beef, wrap well and chill. Toss noodles with ¾ of the sauce to keep them moist. At dinnertime put them on a platter, add the beef, pour on the remaining quarter of the reserved sauce and then decorate.

Serves 4

LENTILS AND EGGPLANT

This can be served as a tasty vegetarian dish or can be included as part of a multi-course dinner. Any kind of lentils can be used, but red lentils cook the fastest. If you use these, don't soak them first before cooking.

Not a particularly attractive-looking dish, it is however a tasty one. Remember it's important not to overcook it. Once the eggplant and lentils are blended at the end, heat and simmer until tender. If you cook this dish too long it becomes 'mushy'.

1 cup lentils	*1 chili, seeded and cut into small pieces*
salt	*¼ cup (2 fl oz) water*
8 small eggplant (about 500 g/1 lb)	*1 tbsp lemon juice 1 tsp sugar*
1 tbsp oil	*3 tsp fish sauce*
2 cloves finely-chopped garlic	*12 mint leaves cut into fine shreds*

Put the lentils into a bowl, cover with boiling water and leave standing for several hours. Drain, rinse and cook in a pan, well-covered with water, until tender. Drain.

Cut the eggplant into halves lengthwise, then quarters, and then into chunky bite-sized pieces. Scatter with salt, stand about 30 minutes, then rinse and drain.

Heat oil, add garlic and chili, and fry until aromatic. Add eggplant and cook for about 5 minutes, or until it has almost softened.

Mix in lentils, about ¼ cup water, lemon juice, sugar and fish sauce. Cook very gently for about 3 minutes until it is hot, and both eggplant and lentils are tender. If you want to prepare any of this in advance, the lentils and eggplant can be precooked, but keep them separate. Warm together gently at dinnertime.

Mix the mint leaves through at the last moment and then serve immediately while they are fragrant and fresh in the dish.   Serves 4

VIETNAM

Well-known American food writer for the *New York Times*, Craig Claiborne, hailed Vietnamese cuisine as 'among the most outstanding on earth'. Vietnamese cooking is distinctive in both flavour and presentation. The latter is considered just as important as the taste. Many dishes are served wrapped in lettuce leaves with a sprig of mint tucked inside, along with a slice of cucumber and carrot. These bundles are then dipped in various sauces.

Where soy is the universal Chinese seasoning, nuoc mam, a salty, pungent fish sauce, is the mainstay of Vietnamese cuisine. Less oil is used than in most Chinese cooking. Vietnamese food is more likely to be simmered or steamed, and only a small amount of thickening is used, so the overall impression is one of freshness and lightness.

Food of each region is distinctive. The cuisine of South Vietnam, with its humid climate, is most frequently encountered in the Vietnamese restaurants which have been opened by Vietnamese refugees in countries throughout the world.

Ingredients are easy to buy, demand creating supply. Spices and sauces are available in Asian shops and in large supermarkets and department stores. Lemon grass and Vietnamese hot mint are grown to supply markets, and roots can be bought from local nurseries.

Vietnamese meals are served in a rice bowl, Chinese-style, although many of the wrapped dishes can only be eaten using fingers. You can serve all the dishes at once or one after the other, so they keep hot.

Accompany the main course with rice, except when a noodle dish forms the bulk of the recipe. Have the traditional nuoc mam in a bowl on the table and, for Vietnamese finger foods, don't forget to have plenty of table napkins on hand. Due to the French influence, bread is often served with Vietnamese meals.

CREAMED CORN CHICKEN SOUP

Corn soup is one of the most popular soups with Westerners, on Chinese menus. It is a rather thick and substantial soup, but the Vietnamese version, while still tasting of corn and chicken, is a little lighter. It can be prepared the day beforehand, with the egg white being added only when reheating.

½ chicken, about 375 g (12 oz)	*1 large clove garlic, crushed*
4 cups (32 fl oz) chicken stock	*1 can 440 g (1 lb) creamed corn*
2 cups (16 fl oz) water	*1 tbsp fish sauce*
¼ tsp salt	*2 egg whites*
1 tbsp oil	*¼ cup finely-chopped spring onion*

Put the chicken into a saucepan with stock and water, seasoning with salt. Bring slowly to the boil, cover and simmer gently for about 1 hour, or until the chicken is very tender.

Leave to cool, and refrigerate. Remove all the fat from the top and take out the chicken. Peel away the skin and pull the flesh into shreds, or cut into small pieces.

Heat oil in a saucepan, add garlic and stir over the heat until aromatic. Don't let it colour.

Mix in the stock, corn and fish sauce and bring to the boil.

Beat the egg whites in a bowl. Tip into the soup, stirring with a fork. It will set in little threads throughout. Scatter on spring onion just before serving.

BEEF BALLS

Known as one of Vietnam's national dishes, finely-ground beef is formed into round balls and served in soup, as a main course, or as a snack. In Vietnam there are restaurants that serve nothing but beef balls.

Vietnamese say the meat should be pounded by hand to a paste, but a food processor does the job very well. It is better to do it this way, rather than buying minced beef from the butcher. This will not be fine enough.

The water in which the beef balls are cooked is seasoned and then served as a soup, with about 5 or more balls in the top of each serve. For a better flavour, I use stock to cook the beef balls. This results in a much richer dish.

---

*500g (1 lb) beef, such as chuck
    steak
1 tbsp water
1 tbsp fish sauce
2 tsp cornflour (cornstarch)
½ tsp baking powder
1 tsp sesame oil
¼ tsp ground black pepper*

*½ tsp sugar
3 cups beef stock or water
finely-chopped spring onion (to
    garnish)
dipping sauces (chili and garlic
    sauce, black bean sauce or hoisin
    sauce)*

Cut the beef into cubes and remove all fat or gristle. Mix with water, fish sauce, cornflour, baking powder, sesame oil, pepper and sugar, and stir to coat the meat. Chill for several hours.

Mince in a food processor in batches, and chill again unless cooking immediately or forming into balls.

To make the meatballs, lightly oil the palm of your left hand and take a tiny piece of meat and put it into this. Close your hand and squeeze. The meat will come out the top and form a round ball about the size of a walnut. You can leave these a short time on some wet plastic wrap, and refrigerate them.

When ready to cook, heat 3 cups light beef stock or water. Season it. Drop the beef balls into this using wet hands or a wet spoon to pick them up. When they turn white and bob to the surface give them a couple more minutes cooking time.

Remove with a slotted spoon. Skim any froth from the liquid. Add another 2 cups water and simmer gently for about 5 minutes. The beef balls can be refrigerated in this water, and stored for a day or reheated in it.

To serve bring the soup to the boil, put the beef balls into bowls with some spring onions and pour the liquid over to generously cover. The balls are taken out and dipped in the sauces, and the soup is drunk at the same time.

Serves 6–8

STIR-FRIED SPINACH

This wouldn't necessarily be made with spinach in Vietnam. Any leafy green vegetable could be used, and the same applies here. I have used spinach but silver beet goes equally well. The whole dish should take only a minute, as it is important to keep a fresh crunchy texture.

1 bunch spinach (500g/1 lb)	*3 tsp fish sauce*
2 tbsp oil	*2 tbsp water*
2 cloves garlic, left whole	*1 egg*
pinch sugar	

Wash the spinach (or other greens) well, and remove any tough stalks. Shred it finely. Heat the oil and add the garlic, frying until lightly coloured. Remove. This will flavour the oil.

Mix the sugar with the fish sauce and water, and beat the egg a little. Put the spinach into the hot oil, and toss for about 30 seconds. Add the fish sauce and water mixture and stir-fry for another 30 seconds or until hot. Stir in the egg quickly and toss. It will bind the mixture.

Serve immediately, before the spinach becomes too soft. Taste for seasoning and add some pepper, if you wish, or a little more salt.

Serves 4

A SIMPLE SALAD OF CHICKEN AND MINT

Vietnamese mint has a stripy leaf, and a pungent flavour not dissimilar to that of coriander but with a hot taste. Like coriander, it may not be popular with everybody, so use with discretion or else use the ordinary common mint. Either way, it is an easy, very fresh- tasting salad which can be served as a main meal, with salad accompaniments such as cucumber, green salad and crusty bread or a rice salad.

If you don't have any chicken stock in which to cook the chicken, use water; it won't be quite as flavoursome but still very good.

2 whole chicken legs, or 4 if small	*½ chili, seeds removed and flesh*
3 cups (24 fl oz) chicken stock	*cut up small*
pinch salt	*1 tbsp sugar*
2 cloves garlic, left whole	*black pepper*
1 white or Spanish-style onion	*salt if needed*
¼ cup (2 fl oz) white wine vinegar	*2 tbsp finely-chopped fresh mint*

Rinse and pat dry the chicken legs. Heat stock or water with salt and garlic. When it comes to the boil add chicken. Let simmer gently, covered, for about 20 minutes, depending on the size of the chicken. Turn off heat and let it stand in the liquid 20 minutes.

Drain but retain liquid, and peel away skin and any fat. (The liquid can be frozen and used again.) Shred the meat and store refrigerated, well-covered to keep it moist.

Cut the onion into very thin rings and add vinegar, chilli and sugar. Stand about 1 hour and drain well. Rinse.

Mix chicken with pepper, salt and mint and toss gently. Lastly, add drained onion rings and serve on a bed of lettuce, with a few sprigs of mint to garnish.

Serves 4

VIETNAMESE SALAD

This particular salad is featured on most Vietnamese restaurant menus, and has dozens of variations. It can include prawns, cooked pork or jellyfish, which is not slippery and soft as you may imagine, but deliciously crunchy and not at all fishy. This version is a simple one.

Serve it as a summer meal or as the first course of a buffet. It is usually served with a bowl of prawn crackers — you simply heap the salad on a prawn cracker and eat it straight away, with a garnish of springs of mint.

---

2 chicken breasts, left on the bone

1 large onion, cut into halves and
   finely sliced

¼ cup white vinegar

½ tsp salt

2 tbsp sugar

1 small cucumber

3 cups very finely shredded cabbage

1 medium-sized grated carrot

1 tbsp fish sauce

1 tbsp water

1 small chili, seeded and finely
   diced

2 cloves garlic, crushed

1 tbsp finely chopped mint

$^1/_3$ cup dry roasted peanuts, finely
   chopped

Put the chicken into a saucepan, cover with water and lightly salt. Bring gently to a boil and let simmer for about 7 minutes (or 10 minutes if the chicken breasts are very thick through). Turn off the heat, and let the chicken cool in the liquid for about 30 minutes. Then refrigerate, still in the liquid to keep the chicken moist. Remove and pull into thin shreds — it will come away from the bone easily.

Place the onion slices into a bowl, add vinegar, season with salt and a little sugar and marinate for 30 minutes.

Peel the cucumber, cut into halves lengthwise and remove seeds. Slice thinly. Mix the cabbage, cucumber, carrot and the fish sauce with a tablespoon of water, add the chili, chicken and garlic, and stir well, adding the well-drained onion slices. Stir in mint, and refrigerate. You can leave this for several hours but not too long or the cabbage will wilt too much. Scatter chopped nuts over the salad when serving.

Serves 4

LETTUCE PARCELS

The Vietnamese love wrapping food in little bundles, either hot dishes like their spring rolls, or salads or cold meat. This is a light and pretty dish and could be served either as a lunch dish or as a first course on a summer's evening.

250 g (8 oz) fillet of pork, well trimmed of any fat or sinew

2 cloves garlic, sliced

6 slices fresh ginger

6 slices of lemon grass

¼ tsp black ground pepper

1 tbsp fish sauce

½ cup cucumber, cut into thin strips (minus the seeds)

½ cup grated carrot

several mint leaves for each parcel

6 large leaves of a soft lettuce (e.g. butter lettuce)

6 green ends of spring onions

Put the fillet of pork into a saucepan with garlic, ginger, lemon grass, pepper and fish sauce. Add water to come to the top of the meat and bring gently to the boil. Cover and simmer on a low heat for about 25 minutes, or until the meat is cooked. Let cool slightly in the liquid and then wrap and store refrigerated. Cut into fine slices.

Mix cucumber and carrot together.

Put lettuce on a bench and arrange some pork slices, a little mound of the cucumber and carrot and several mint leaves, and wrap over to enclose, placing them join-side down. If you can't get large enough lettuce leaves use several overlapping leaves to make the parcels.

Put the spring onion tops into a shallow container. Pour boiling water over the top and let stand for about a minute, so they soften. Drain and rinse with cold water to retain the green colour. Use one of these to tie up each parcel. If the spring onion is thick, I split them through the centre to make a neater tie.

Cover with some plastic wrap and refrigerate if not serving immediately. You can store them about 6 hours.

Serve with a bowl of nuoc mam (see page 43).

Makes about 6

TOMATOES STUFFED WITH BEAN CURD

This stuffed tomato dish can be made with cooked meat, such as pork, mixed with fish sauce and spring onions in the centre. But this version is a vegetarian one, very light yet high in protein.

4 medium-sized ripe tomatoes	*salt if required to taste*
2 large Chinese mushrooms	*1 clove garlic, crushed*
185g (4 oz) bean curd	*1 tbsp fish sauce*
2 tbsp finely-chopped spring onion	*¼ tsp sugar*
¼ tsp black pepper	*1 tbsp oil (to cook tomatoes)*

Cut tomatoes into halves, remove the seedy section and discard. Turn over to drain on a plate. Cover the mushrooms with hot water and let soak 20 minutes. Drain, remove the stalks and cut the caps into small dice.

Mash the bean curd with a fork, add all the remaining ingredients, and mix well. Fill the tomato halves, smoothing the top.

Heat the oil in a pan, put tomatoes in, stuffed-side down, and cook about 10 minutes over a gentle heat. Carefully turn them over and cook another 3 minutes on the other side, or until just softened. Don't let them break up.

Serve with a little parsley or leaves of coriander on top, if you wish.

Serves 4

CHICKEN IN SPICY TOMATO SAUCE

Best made when you can get flavoursome tomatoes. Be sure to add all the pepper to this dish as this is what gives the sauce its interesting spiciness.

4 chicken breasts, boned and
   skinned

2 tbsp oil

1 large onion, cut into halves and
   thinly sliced

3 cloves garlic, crushed

4 large tomatoes, peeled and
   roughly diced

1 bay leaf

1 tsp sugar

1 tsp black peppercorns

½ cup (4 fl oz) water

2 tsp fish sauce

Cut the chicken breasts into large bite-sized cubes. Warm the oil in a saucepan, large frying pan or wok, and add the onion. Sauté over moderate heat for a few minutes, then add the garlic and chicken. Sauté again, turning the chicken pieces over, then remove them from the pan.

Mix in all the remaining ingredients, and bring to the boil. Simmer gently for about 3 minutes, or until you have a thickish sauce.

Return the chicken pieces and cook over low heat for another 3 minutes, or until the chicken pieces are cooked. Be careful not to overcook them.

This dish can be reheated, but do so very gently or the chicken breast becomes dry.

Serves 4

CHICKEN WITH LEMON GRASS AND CHILI

Lemon grass, garlic and chili are an important part of the Vietnamese repertoire of seasonings, and chicken has a particular affinity with the aromatic and fresh flavour of lemon grass. Buy the fresh stalks if you can; the dried stalks have very little taste. It's better to substitute grated lemon rind if you can't obtain fresh lemon grass.

1 chicken, 1.5 kg (3 lb)

1 stalk lemon grass

1 large clove garlic, finely chopped

2 tbsp fish sauce

¼ tsp black ground pepper

2 tbsp oil

1 large onion, cut into halves and then into tiny strips or segments

1 tsp finely-chopped chili, minus seeds

½ cup (4 fl oz) water

Cut the chicken into small portions. It can be boned, if you wish, although the portions of bone add flavour. Rinse to make sure there are no scraps of bone, and pat dry.

Cut the tough top from the lemon grass and remove the tough outside layers. Finely chop the white inside part.

In a bowl, mix the garlic, fish sauce and pepper. Add the chicken and lemon grass, stir to coat, and let marinate for about 30 minutes.

Heat oil in a wok or frying pan. Add the onion, and stir until slightly softened. Then add the chili, followed by the chicken. Cook the chicken over high heat, turning it over until it has changed colour.

Add the water, and turn to low. Cook about 25 minutes, turning every so often. You can partly-cover with a lid if the liquid is evaporating too much. Serve as soon as the chicken is cooked.

Serves 4

GRILLED CHICKEN ON SKEWERS

This easy dish has more of a Chinese influence than most Vietnamese cooking. (Soy sauce is used in Vietnam but nowhere near to the same extent as in China.) It can be cooked under a kitchen griller (broiler) or on a barbecue.

500 g (1 lb) boned, skinned
   chicken breast
2 tbsp oil
2 tsp finely-chopped shallots
3 cloves crushed garlic
¼ cup (2 fl oz) dry sherry

1 tbsp water
½ tsp five spice powder
1 tsp sugar
2 tsp soy sauce
1 tsp fish sauce

Put some bamboo skewers into a shallow dish and cover with water. Cut the chicken into small cubes, about 2.5 cm x 2.5 cm. Put into a bowl.

Heat the oil and add all the remaining ingredients. Bring gently to the boil. Remove and cool slightly. Pour this mixture over the chicken, and turn over to make sure all the pieces are coated. Cover and marinate, refrigerated, for several hours.

Remove and put the chicken pieces on the bamboo skewers and grill or barbecue the chicken, turning over frequently and brushing several times with the marinade. Be careful not to overcook. Once marinated, it seems to cook more quickly.

Serve with some lettuce which can be used to wrap up the pieces of chicken for eating.

Serves 4

CHICKEN CURRY

As in most Asian countries, curried food is frequently served in Vietnam. The difference with a Vietnamese curry is in the use of fragrant lemon grass. The original versions have a lot more oil and coconut milk. I have reduced these considerably.

1 chicken, about 1.5 kg (3 lb)	*3 cloves chopped garlic*
1½ tbsp curry powder	*2 onions, cut into thin wedge*
¼ tsp black pepper ground	*shaped sections and separated*
1 tsp sugar	*1 bay leaf*
¼ tsp salt, or to taste	*1 stalk lemon grass, finely chopped*
2 tbsp oil	*1 cup (8 fl oz) water, or chicken*
2 sweet potatoes, peeled and cut	*stock*
into bite-sized cubes	*¼ cup (2 fl oz) coconut milk*
1 additional tbsp oil	

Cut the chicken into very small portions. Mix the curry with pepper, sugar, salt and rub into the skin of the chicken. Leave several hours.

Heat the oil, add sweet potatoes and brown lightly, turning frequently. Remove and add the extra oil and garlic, onions, bay leaf, lemon grass and chicken pieces. Fry until they have changed colour, add water, and simmer gently for about 15 minutes or until the chicken is partly tender.

Return the potatoes to the pan with the coconut milk, and cook gently covered for another 15 minutes or until both the chicken and potato are tender.

Taste. Season with a little salt, if necessary.

Serves 4

SPICY GRILLED QUAIL

Chicken is the poultry used most frequently in Vietnamese cooking, but occasionally you will find recipes for pigeon and quail. This is one of the nicest of the quail dishes. The marinade flavours the commercial birds, which can often do with a boost, and keeps the flesh moist, while the grilling lends a lovely, crunchy coating and colour to the skin. If you don't want to serve this as a main meal, you could serve a little quail each as a first course, for an exotic change.

8 quail

2 tbsp oil

4 crushed cloves garlic

2 tbsp finely-chopped shallot

2 tbsp finely chopped lemon grass

1 tsp chili oil, finely chopped fresh chili or a dash of cayenne

1 tbsp sugar

2 tbsp fish sauce

Cut each quail down the backbone; don't cut through the breast. Turn over on the board and press down to flatten the birds.

Put the oil, garlic, shallot and lemon grass into a pot and warm gently until it comes to the boil. Remove from the heat and add the chili, sugar and fish sauce.

Put a little of this mixture into a shallow dish, arrange the quail on it, and then spread the remainder of the mixture over the top. Cover and let marinate for a couple of hours.

Have a griller (broiler) pre-heated and grill the quail until browned on both sides, turning the birds over a couple of times.

Serves 4

PORK COOKED IN FISH SAUCE

Belly pork is best of all for this dish, but it can be rather fatty. So you may prefer to use a portion of well-trimmed leg pork. This dish has a very good flavour, reheats well and makes a nice meal served with rice and mixed salad.

500 g (1 lb) belly pork or leg pork	*1 tbsp sugar*
1 tbsp oil	*1 tbsp fish sauce*
1 large onion, cut into halves and	*¼ tsp black pepper*
* then into thin wedges*	*salt to taste*
3 cloves garlic, sliced	

Cut the pork into cubes about 3.5 cm x 3.5 cm (1½ in. x 1½ in.). Heat the oil in a pan, add the onion, and cook, tossing for a few minutes. Add the garlic and scatter sugar over the top. Stir with the onions until they are tinged with colour. Add the pork. When all the pork has been added and the pot is very hot, add water to barely come to the top of the meat.

Bring to the boil, stirring to get up any browned bits from the base, and then add the fish sauce. Skim the top if any froth forms, and cook over the lowest heat for an hour, turning the pork pieces over once during this time. Have the pan partly covered with a lid.

Towards the end of the cooking time, when the pork is almost tender, remove the lid and let the liquid reduce down to just a small amount of juice. Add pepper last and stir through the sauce. Taste for salt.

Serves 4

RICH BEEF SOUP WITH NOODLES

Combinations with noodles are a major part of Vietnamese soups, and this particular one is served in a large, deep bowl, as a meal to be enjoyed at any time of the day. Although pork and fish are often featured, beef is the most common ingredient.

500g (1lb) stewing beef	*1 onion, cut into halves*
500g (1lb) beef shanks, cut into pieces	*pinch cayenne pepper*
	1 tbsp sugar
6 slices fresh ginger	*1 tbsp fish sauce*
3 cloves garlic	*250g (8oz) fresh egg noodles (or dried if you can't obtain fresh)*
1 stalk chopped lemon grass	
1 bay leaf	*8 spring onions, finely chopped*
1 star anise	*125g (4oz) bean shoots*
1 cinnamon stick	*sprigs of coriander to garnish*

Cut the beef into large pieces, discarding any fat, and put into a large pan with the shanks. Add the ginger, garlic, lemon grass, bay leaf, star anise, cinnamon, onion and cayenne pepper. Bring slowly to the boil, skim the top occasionally.

Add sugar and fish sauce and put a lid on top to partly cover. Let simmer very gently a couple of hours, or until the meat is tender. This can be done days beforehand. Refrigerate until needed, and remove any fat from the top before re-heating. Add salt, if necessary.

Cook the noodles in lightly-salted boiling water until just tender, and drain.

Have 6 warm bowls ready, and put some spring onion, bean sprouts and a little of the beef into each. It is nicest if you shred the meat first rather than leaving it in big chunks.

Divide the noodles among them, and then when the soup is boiling hot, pour over the top. Scatter the top with a few leaves of coriander and serve immediately with a bowl of nuoc mam on the table.

Serves 6

NUOC MAM

Nuoc mam is a dip based on fish sauce which is served with almost everything in Vietnam. You dip food in it and spoon it over dishes. No meal would be considered complete without a little bowl of this on the table. It is both hot, sweet, sour and pungent — all at the same time. The amount of chili and garlic can be adjusted, if you wish.

1 fresh red chili, seeded and cut
   into tiny pieces
1 clove garlic, crushed
2 tsp sugar, or to taste

2 tbsp fish sauce
2 tbsp water
2 tbsp lemon juice

Put the chili into a bowl and add all the remaining ingredients. Then taste, remembering it won't be quite as strong when used as a sauce as when you taste it straight.

Sometimes a tablespoon of grated carrot is added to the sauce. A tablespoon of finely-chopped or ground roasted peanuts is another nice addition. It can be kept for a day in the refrigerator, but must be very well covered or everything will smell of nuoc mam.

JAPAN

Of all Asian cuisines, Japanese is one of the healthiest, because it contains only tiny amounts of fat. Few dishes are fried, and fish, tofu, (bean curd), and sea vegetables are prominently featured, along with such seasonings as soy and miso (fermented soy bean paste).

However, the salt and sugar content is high. I have modified this a little, although it is not possible to change it too much without upsetting the balance of flavours. It is essential to the Japanese that their food is ultra-fresh, and is cooked simply, to let the ingredients reveal their individual character and beauty.

Artistic and elegant presentation in the arrangement of food expresses the Japanese respect for nature; its inspiration is reflected in their meals. Take your own cue from nature when preparing Japanese dishes, and add texture and flavour with garnishes — scatter finely-chopped green onion shreds over fish or noodles. Seasonal flowers or leaves can also be used or simply add some beautifully-cut lemon slices or carrot shreds.

The following dishes can be cooked separately, or combined to form a simple dinner. Soup could be followed by a salad, then a dish of meat, fish or chicken, served with rice. Tea and fruit could finish the meal. Rice is considered an important food, and other dishes are meant to complement it. For the best balance, when selecting dishes to serve, make sure you don't choose ones cooked by the same method.

In Japan, salads, served in tiny portions, are used either as a tiny appetiser or they may be presented at the end of the meal. There are two main types of salad: those with a vinegar base, and those with tofu, miso or, occasionally, sesame as a base. These are not meant to be served in large portions, as a Western salad would be. The best way to enjoy them is to serve them exquisitely-arranged in tiny portions on little plates.

There is no need to buy any special equipment for these dishes. Although there are several special items used in a traditional Japanese kitchen — such as sushi-rice tubs, rice paddles and sushi mats — the dishes in this section can easily be prepared with items found in the average Western kitchen.

A glossary of ingredients used in Japanese cooking is included at the end of this chapter.

DASHI (ICHIBANO)

This is the equivalent of stock in Western cooking, important to
Japanese cuisine as a main flavouring ingredient and also the base for
soups, dipping sauces and vegetable dishes. It is sometimes called
bonito. You can buy instant dashi (available in either liquid or
powdered form). But the home-made version is even better, and quite
simple to make.

1 piece of dried kelp, about 10 cm	*4 cups (32 fl oz) water*
(4 in.)	*1 cup bonito flakes (shaved fish)*

Wipe the kelp with a damp cloth. Never wash it, or the flavour is lost.
Cut into about 8 pieces to release the flavour as it cooks. Put into a
saucepan with 3½ cups of cold water and bring to the boil over a
medium-low heat.

When the mixture is just beginning to bubble, take the pan away
from the heat and remove the kelp. If it is still tough the flavour may
not be yet released and you may have to cook a little longer. Always
keep the mixture just below the boil. (If cooking too fast, add a little
more cold water.)

Add another half cup of water and bonito. Heat again. As soon as it
comes to the boil, take off the heat. (If you let stock boil with bonito
in it, the flavour is bitter.)

Leave until the flakes sink to the base. Pour through a sieve lined
with a damp piece of cheese-cloth or thin cloth. Don't press down on
the bonito flakes. The liquid will be clear and golden.

It can be kept refrigerated for about a week.

Makes 4 cups of dashi

TERRIYAKI

Terriyaki means shining grill. The dark marinade forms a glaze on top as well as flavouring the food. There are a number of these popular terriyaki dishes. Meat can be served wrapped around vegetables and fried with the sauce. There is also a preparation for fish, firstly marinated and then grilled or sautéed with the sauce. Beef terriyaki is the best known version of all.

¼ cup (2 fl oz) soy sauce

2 tbsp sugar

4 thick pieces grilling steak

1 tbsp oil

¼ cup (2 fl oz) sake

6 spring onions, finely chopped

1½ cups bean shoots

vegetable oil

Mix the soy sauce with the sugar first, then stir. Leave to stand for about 5 minutes, for the sugar to dissolve.

Heat just enough oil to film the base of a frying pan. Sauté the steaks over very high heat until brown on both sides. Pour the sake over the top and turn the heat to low. Cover and cook gently for about 2 minutes. If the steaks are very thick you may need to cook a little longer.

Remove the meat to a warmed platter.

Add the soy and sugar and cook until glazed. Return the steaks and any juices to the pan, and turn steaks over several times until they are coated with the shining sauce.

Separately, in another pan, heat a spoonful of oil. Add the spring onions and bean shoots and cook over high heat for about a minute, tossing.

Serve the steaks on a plate with the spring onion and bean shoot mixture on the side.

Serves 4

CHICKEN SOUP WITH LEEKS

250 g (½ lb) boned chicken breast

4 baby leeks, or 3 medium-sized
  leeks

4 cups (32 fl oz) chicken stock

1 tbsp light soy sauce

1 tbsp mirin

lemon juice

a few slivers of lemon rind

a few fine slivers of green ginger

Cut the chicken breast into about 18 pieces, removing the skin and any fat. Chop off the root end of the leeks, and wash well. Cut them into halves lengthwise (or into quarters, if they are large), and then across into diagonal pieces.

Bring the stock to the boil. Add the leek and chicken pieces and simmer very gently for about 10 minutes, or until they are both partly tender. Add the soy and mirin, then taste. Adding salt only if necessary. Cook another few minutes, or until the leeks and chicken are tender. Remove both of these.

Strain the soup. If there is any fat on top, place some paper towelling on it. Lift off, and the fat will stick to the paper.

Add some lemon juice to taste. Mix in the ginger and lemon rind pieces and let them sit in the hot liquid for a few minutes to soften. Return the chicken and leek to the liquid. Reheat if they are cool.

When serving, it is best if you scoop out the chicken and leeks and divide them evenly. Then top up with the soup.

Serves 4

MINCED CHICKEN LOAF

⅓ cup finely-chopped spring onions	1 tsp soy sauce
⅓ cup finely-chopped leek	2 tsp sake
500 g (1 lb) finely-minced chicken	1 egg
2 tsp grated ginger	1 tbsp sesame seeds
1 tsp sugar	

Combine everything except for the sesame seeds. Mix well with your hands until smooth, and leave in the refrigerator for about 30 minutes so the flavours can blend.

Cut out a circle of non-stick paper to fit into the base of a round cake tin about 20 cm (8 in.) in size. Brush this lightly with some oil and fit into the base. Put the chicken on top and spread out to form an even layer, flattening with a damp hand. Scatter the top with sesame seeds. Bake in a moderate oven (180°C/350°F) for about 18–20 minutes, or until firm to touch.

Leave 5 minutes before turning out, then invert right side up onto a heated serving platter. Cut into slices or wedges.

It can be decorated with spring onions if you wish.

Serves 4

RICE TOPPED WITH CHICKEN AND EGG

The Japanese name for this dish, Oyako Domburi, means parent and child, denoting the relationship between the chicken and the egg. A 'dombu' is a dish of rice topped with something else — it could be meat, an omelette or fish. This dish is rather soft and light to eat, and it has a lovely flavour. The sticky rice becomes moist with the juices. The chicken and egg rest on top.

2 cups rice	*1 tbsp sugar*
4 cups (32 fl oz) water	*¼ cup diced spring onion*
250g (8 oz) boned chicken	*4 eggs*
2 cups (16 fl oz) dashi	*a tiny bunch of trefoil, if in season*
4 tbsp soy sauce	*1 tbsp pickled ginger, cut into fine strips*

Rinse the rice several times. Leave to soak in water for 30 minutes. Then put it into a large saucepan. Bring to the boil, then reduce heat so it just simmers gently. Cook, covered, for 15 minutes.

Turn off the heat and let it sit another 15 minutes. Mix gently with a wet wooden spatula.

Dice the chicken into small bite-sized pieces. Mix dashi, soy and sugar and bring to the boil in a saucepan.

Add the diced chicken and trefoil, then cover the pan. Turn off the heat and leave to stand for 5 minutes. The chicken will be cooked.

Add spring onions. Beat the egg and bring the mixture in the pan to the boil again. Pour eggs over the top. When the edges bubble, swirl with chopsticks, once only, and take off the heat. Leave aside a few minutes. It will thicken more in the heat of the pan.

To serve, place the rice in deep bowls and spoon out a portion of the egg and chicken over the top. Put some strips of ginger in the centre. Serve immediately.

It can be decorated with some shreds of nori or left plain.   Serves 4

TOFU ON SKEWERS

The Japanese for this dish is Tofu Dengaku, the word 'dengaku' referring to traditional open air fairs that were held in the temple grounds, a mixture of entertainment and agricultural displays. In this holiday atmosphere there were always stilt dancers, and this popular roadside snack was named after puppets because of its resemblance to the stiff-legged stilt walkers.

It is a simple idea. Slices of grilled tofu (bean curd) are covered with gaily coloured spreads, based on miso paste, on top. The topping preparation does take some time, but it can be done well in advance.

Tofu Dengaku is traditionally served on two-pronged skewers but if you are unable to buy these, a couple of short bamboo skewers make a good substitute.

You will need 1 kg (2 lb) of tofu for this recipe.

BASIC MISO TOPPING

1 cup (8 fl oz) white miso	2 tbsp sake
2 tbsp sugar	2 tbsp mirin
½ cup (4 fl oz) dashi	3 egg yolks
2 tbsp dashi	

Mix all the ingredients except the yolks in a basin. Beat these and add last. Then stand the basin over a pan of hot water. It should be just above the water level. Cook until thick, giving it an occasional stir. Don't let the mixture come to the boil or it will curdle. Divide into three bowls.

ADDITIONS FOR MISO

2 tsp ginger juice	pinch of tea powder
1 tbsp red miso	drop of green good colouring

Add ginger juice and red miso to a second bowl, add the pinch of tea powder and colouring to the third bowl.

Cover and chill if not using immediately.

The filling may not look firm enough to spread at this stage, but it thickens more as it cools.

GARNISH

Fine shreds of lemon rind, cooked until slightly softened, herb leaves (e.g. parsley, basil or coriander) and sansho (Japanese pepper condiment).

TO ASSEMBLE
1 kg (2 lb) of tofu

Wrap the tofu in a piece of muslin or a kitchen towel and put a plate on top, to weight it slightly.

Let it rest for 1 hour, to remove some excess water.

Cut into rectangular pieces. Tofu can vary in shape, so it is sensible to cut it according to whether or not it is a square piece. The sections should be about 5 cm x 2.5 cm (2 in. x 1 in.).

Refrigerate on a plate if not using immediately.

TO FINISH

Insert a fork or bamboo skewers into the long part of the tofu. Grill over charcoal or under a pre-heated griller on a flat baking tray for about 3 minutes on each side, or until the tofu is speckled with brown.

Spread topping over each portion of tofu, using the three different toppings. Smooth the edges with a wet knife.

Decorate with the different garnishes and return to the griller until the topping has heated through. It takes about a minute.

Serve as soon as they are cooked.

YUAN-STYLE GRILLED FISH

The marinade gives an attractive colour and glaze to the fish, and the generous amount of sake makes it moist. It can be steamed instead of grilled. This recipe is supposedly the creation of a great Japanese gourmet, Kitamura Yuan.

I find it successful with any fish which has been filleted and is of medium texture. However, it is not a good way to cook cutlets of fish, because the outside becomes dry before the cutlets have cooked through to the bone.

---

500 g (1 lb) fish fillets	*⅓ cup (2⅔ fl oz) soy sauce*
3 tsp salt	*½ cup (4 fl oz) mirin*
½ cup (4 fl oz) sake	*4 thin slices lemon*

Pat the fish dry and sprinkle it with salt on both sides. Place in a shallow china or glass dish and leave it to stand for about an hour. Now rinse the fish, or the salt taste will be too strong. Pat dry again. Put back into the dish.

Mix the sake with soy and mirin. Cut the lemons into a few pieces and put over the fish with the sake mixture. Leave for 30 minutes, turning the fish over once if it is not covered by the marinade. Drain and pat dry.

Score the skin through at intervals of about ½ cm (¼ in.). If you are using skinless fish, score very lightly or the fish may break. If it is a thin fillet, skip this step altogether.

Have a griller (broiler) heated. Put the fish on a flat tray and grill, brushing with the marinade several times, until it flakes with a fork. Don't overcook, I find it takes between 4–6 minutes, depending on the fish and the heat of the griller. You can, of course, cook over hot

coals on a barbecue but you will need to place it on a flat tray, or skewer several pieces together so they won't fall through. If using skewers, pull them out gently so you don't break up the portions of fish.

Serve on some thin slices of lemon. It can be eaten hot, warm or in Japanese style, as a cold dish.

Serves 4

UDON NOODLES

This type of noodle dish is generally served as a separate light meal, without the usual accompaniment of rice. Fat white noodles, either flat or rounded and served steaming in flavoured liquid, make a healthy, delicious dish.

The Japanese for this dish is Namba Udon. Namba, now a bustling, busy district, was once renowned for its wild onion, and dishes with 'Namba' in their name usually feature spring onions, as does this one.

It is served in small deep bowls. First you pick up the noodles with chopsticks, along with bits of chicken and mushroom, and then the liquid is drunk directly from the bowl. If you don't want to do this, spoons could be provided.

500 g fresh noodles

*6 fresh shitake mushrooms or 3
    large dried Chinese mushrooms*

6 cups (48 fl oz) dashi

1 tbsp sugar

1 tbsp soy sauce

*375 g (12 oz) boned skinned
    chicken breast*

½ cup chopped spring onions

SRI LANKA   Spicy Barbecued Fish, p.147, is traditionally cooked in banana leaves.

55

Slice the fresh shitake mushrooms, or else cover the dried mushrooms with warm water and let them soften for 30 minutes.

Remove the tough stalks and slice the caps.

Heat dashi, sugar and soy. Cut the chicken breast into small bite-sized pieces and add to the liquid. Simmer gently for about 5 minutes. Turn off the heat and let it rest.

Bring a large saucepan of water to the boil, and add noodles. Cook over high heat until tender. Taste to check. Add 1 tsp salt to the pan and cover it. Let stand for 3 minutes. Drain the noodles.

Put the noodles into the pan with the liquid and chicken. Heat again, add the spring onions, and cook for a minute. Taste. You can add a little more soy, salt or pepper if the liquid is not sufficiently flavoured.

Put into a large bowl, serve noodles with some chicken and spoon liquid over the top.

Serves 4

GRILLED EGGPLANT

This dish is served at room temperature, rather like a salad. The
Japanese eggplant is long and thin and retains more flavour if grilled
rather than stewed or steamed. You can't make this dish with large
eggplants as they would be too charred on the outside by the time the
insides were tender. Choose firm shining eggplants and retain a tiny
piece of the stalk for appearance.

12 baby eggplants	1 tsp grated ginger
2 tbsp dashi	1 tsp sugar
2 tbsp soy sauce	threads of bonito fish (for garnish)
1 tsp ginger juice	

Brush the side of the eggplants with vegetable oil. With a fine poultry
skewer, make a few holes in the sides, so the heat can penetrate.

Grill over a charcoal grill or under a preheated griller (broiler) until
the outsides are dark and the thickest parts of the eggplants tender
and soft when pressed. You need to turn them frequently so they
cook evenly. The time depends on the heat, but I find they take about
15–20 minutes.

Have a bowl with some iced water ready and drop the hot eggplants
into this to cool. When they are cool enough to handle, carefully peel.
Cut into slices, or leave them attached at the end and slice lengthwise.

Mix the dashi, soy, ginger and sugar and pour over the top.

Garnish with a few threads of bonito flakes when serving, and have
some wedges of lemon on the side.

This is quite a rich dish. A little goes a long way!

Serves 4

RED AND WHITE SALAD

This salad is a mixture of long white radish and carrot shreds, hence the name. An attractive dish, with a nice crispy texture, it is best made well beforehand, so the flavours of the marinade can penetrate. It can be stored for several days in the refrigerator.

1 white radish (about 200–250g/ 6–8 oz)

2 tsp salt

2 medium-sized carrots

½ cup (4 fl oz) rice wine vinegar

2 tbsp mirin

1 tbsp sugar

½ cup (4 fl oz) dashi

half a dozen strips lemon rind.

Peel or scrape off the skin and cut the radish into sections about 5 cm (2 in.) in length.

Slice each one very thinly lengthwise, to make strips. Put these into a bowl and add 1 teaspoon salt. Do the same with the carrot. Let them both stand for 10 minutes and then knead gently with your fingers. Put onto some kitchen paper and press down to get out as much moisture as possible.

Put them both into a bowl. Mix all the remaining ingredients in a saucepan and bring to the boil.

Remove and let it cool. Mix half with the vegetables, stir and stand 1 hour. Drain and press out the liquid. Discard this marinade. Add the remaining half of the marinade and let the vegetables stand in this, covered, in the refrigerator. Before serving the salad, drain it through a sieve again.

Mound it lightly in a bowl for serving.

Serves 8

SPECIAL INGREDIENTS

The following ingredients are among those used in this chapter.

AUBERGINE (Eggplant)
The Japanese variety is long, thin and quite small.

BONITO FLAKES
These packaged flakes are sold as hana-katsuo. They should be very fresh, so buy from a shop with a good turnover. These have a use-by date, but it is usually in Japanese.

BUCKWHEAT NOODLES (Soba)
These are sold dry in packages in Japanese grocery stores, and often in health food shops.

DASHI
A seaweed and fish based stock which is as important in Japanese cooking as is stock in Western cooking. Japanese shops sell the essence to make an instant dashi, but home-made dashi has a fresher taste.

GINGER JUICE
This is quite strong and hot, and the quantity you get depends greatly on the freshness of the ginger root.
   Wash the ginger root and peel it. Finely grate it over a bowl. Tip the grated mixture into a cloth. Squeeze out the juice into a dish from the cloth.

HORSERADISH (Wasabi)
This is sold in tubes or powdered form which is mixed to a paste, like a dry mustard. The tube is easier, and it keeps well. This highly-pungent hot green paste is an essential accompaniment for many raw fish dishes. But be warned: a little goes a long way!

KELP (Konbu)
Dark brownish-green, it is sold dried in packets. Once opened, keep stored in an airtight container at room temperature. This sea vegetable is an important flavouring for dashi.

MIRIN
Although this is a sweet sake, it is sold in grocery stores because the alcohol level is so low.

MISO
This is a soya bean paste which has been fermented, and is used as a base for salad dressings, in soup or as a condiment. It comes in differing consistencies and colours.

NORI
This seaweed is used as a sushi-wrap, and also as a garnish. Rich in protein, calcium, iron and minerals, the better the colour, the higher the vitamin content. Once opened, store in an airtight container. Toast to freshen the flavour by passing over a gas flame several times, or quickly over an electric hotplate set on high.

RADISH (Daikon)
A mild-flavoured radish, generally used raw, this large white vegetable root can also be cooked.

RICE VINEGAR
A mild-flavoured vinegar. You can't substitute a Western vinegar for this, as it would be too harsh.

SAKE
Japanese rice wine.

SANSHO
A peppery spice which comes from the seed pods of a prickly ash tree.

TREFOIL
A member of the parsley family, it has three leaves, hence the name. It can be used coarsely chopped or added whole. Not always easy to find fresh, either omit or substitute a few sprigs of parsley.

CHINA

The Chinese have learnt to treat all kinds of food, even the humblest, with respect and care. In a country where food is sometimes scarce, meals are imaginatively conceived and taken seriously.

China's culinary heritage is long and its range of cuisines is vast. I have not chosen any particular region; rather I have selected individual dishes which have a light, fresh flavour and a minimum of oil and salt. Much Chinese food is stir-fried, using quite a quantity of oil. This has been reduced as has soy sauce, but the balance of the dish has been retained.

Chinese food is best presented on a large platter, so portions can be spooned out over rice in a bowl, or even on a flat dinner plate. You can simply cook one of the dishes as a main course, with rice and a bowl of stir-fried vegetables, or you can cook several dishes to make a multi-course meal — the more traditional way to eat Chinese food.

In particular, I have concentrated on a style of Chinese food which is quick and makes a lovely family meal: tasty without being too expensive or time-consuming.

Most of these dishes can be stir-fried in a wok. Steaming can be done in inexpensive bamboo baskets which you can fit over the wok. If you don't have a wok, a frying pan will do, but it needs to be large enough to be able to toss and stir ingredients without tipping them over the stove.

STEAMED PORK LOAF

A family dish, it can be prepared in advance, reheated, or eaten cold as a sliced loaf. This is a Chinese version of the Western meat loaf, slightly firmer in texture than one made from beef, but infinitely tastier.

500 g (1 lb) finely-minced pork	2 tbsp soy sauce
1 tbsp grated fresh ginger	¼ tsp black ground pepper
1 clove crushed garlic	1 tbsp rice wine
¼ cup finely chopped spring onion, including some of the green tops	2 tsp cornflour
	1 egg white

Put everything into a bowl except for the pork and mix well. Then add the pork and, using your hand, mix thoroughly. I don't usually add salt because the soy is sufficient, but if you like you could cook a tiny piece in a pan, and check for seasonings. Cover and leave refrigerated if not using within 30 minutes. (It can be kept 12 hours at this stage.)

Transfer to a shallow dish — even a cake tin will do — or else form into a round loaf shape and put onto a plate that will fit into a steamer. Smooth the top with a wet hand. Steam over medium high heat for about 15 minutes, then turn down and cook for another 5–10 minutes, depending on the thickness of the pork.

Let rest for 10 minutes before cutting. It will have a little liquid around it. Drain this away unless reheating, in which case retain the liquid, as it will keep the meat moist.

Serves 4 as a main course, or 6–8 as part of a multi-course meal

HOT AND SOUR SOUP

This soup is seen on Peking and Sichuan menus, with differing versions in almost every case. It is also included in most Chinese cook books. Believed to create an appetite, it is sometimes made with pork broth, and at other times with chicken stock. The 'sour' comes from vinegar, and the 'hot' from white pepper — not chili as you may imagine.

Other ingredients include two kinds of mushrooms, fine shreds of pork and velvety cubes of bean curd.

I find this soup makes an excellent light lunch, followed by a salad. Be sure to buy fat-free pork, or make up the soup the day beforehand so you can skim any fat from the top.

---

250 g (8 oz) fillet of pork or a tender low-fat pork cut (e.g a piece from the leg)

1 tsp soy sauce

1 tsp rice wine

½ tsp sugar

6 dried wood ear mushrooms

6 medium-small dried black mushrooms

1 tbsp oil

60 g (2 oz) bamboo shoots, cut into shreds

90 g (3 oz) bean curd, neatly diced

4 cups (32 fl oz) chicken stock

2–3 tbsp red wine vinegar, depending on its strength

1 tbsp soy sauce

½ tsp sesame oil

1 tbsp cornflour mixed with water to make a thin paste

1 tbsp grated fresh ginger

white pepper to taste

2 egg whites

¼ cup finely-chopped spring onion or coriander leaves (Chinese parsley)

Cut the pork into thin strips, about the thickness of a bean and 5 cm (2 in.) in length.

Place in bowl and mix in soy, sugar and rice wine. Leave to marinate for about 30 minutes.

Put both types of mushrooms into another basin, cover with warm water and let soak 30 minutes. Drain mushrooms, remove the tough stalks and cut the caps into strips.

Add oil to a saucepan or wok and toss in pork, stirring to separate the pieces. Cook about a minute.

Add mushrooms, bamboo shoots, bean curd and stir. Mix in stock, vinegar, soy, oil, and bring to a boil. Stir in the cornflour with ginger, and season with pepper.

When it returns to the boil, remove from the heat, cover and let rest for 1 minute to blend flavours. It can be left at this stage for reheating.

At dinnertime, heat the soup and beat the egg whites with a fork for a few seconds, to break up. Add to the boiling soup, stirring with a fork so the whites set in threads. Taste, and adjust the seasoning if necessary with a little more pepper and a few more drops of vinegar or, if too sharp, a little extra chicken stock.

Serve scattered with the spring onions or coriander.

Serves 4

CHICKEN STOCK

This is an important part of any Chinese meal. Traditionally, a big pot of stock is left on the table so diners can ladle in a small cupful as a drink from time to time. This basic stock is not only important for soup. It is also useful to store in the refrigerator so you can add additional flavour to many different Asian dishes.

500 g (1 lb) chicken necks or giblets
½ chicken, cut into quarters, or some chicken bones or wing tips

3 thick slices fresh ginger, peeled
1 large onion, cut into quarters
2 peeled, whole cloves garlic

Wash the chicken pieces and drain. Put them into a large saucepan with remaining ingredients, and cover with water. (It usually takes about 5–6 cups.) Slowly bring to the boil, skimming the top occasionally, and partly cover. Cook over the lowest possible heat for about 3 hours.

Let cool slightly, and pour through a strainer. Chill, leaving the layer of fat on top while storing (this helps keep it better), but remove before using.

It can be kept refrigerated for 4 days. After this it is best to boil up again and return to the refrigerator, or to freeze the stock.

SPICY MARINATED CUCUMBER

This piquant salad can be served as a vegetable accompaniment to meats, and is also great as an appetiser or hors-d'oeuvre.

If you don't like your food too hot, you could use only half a chili instead of the whole chili in the ingredients below, adding a few drops of Tabasco Sauce.

1 long cucumber (or 2 if they are small)	1 tsp Sichuan pepper
2 tsp salt	2 tbsp sugar
1 finely-chopped chili, seeds removed	2 tbsp white vinegar
	2 tsp water

Peel cucumber and slice it very thinly. Put into a bowl and add the salt, mixing with your hands so the cucumber is well coated. Let this mixture stand for about 30 minutes. Then rinse, and drain well. By now, the cucumber should have softened.

Mix the chili with pepper and put into a dry pan, heating gently and stirring with a fork until it smells quite spicy.

Remove to a small saucepan and add all the remaining ingredients. Heat until it comes to a boil.

Place the cucumber in a bowl and pour the marinade over the top through a sieve (to get rid of the chili and large bits of pepper). Leave it to marinate for at least 8 hours — it is even better if left overnight.

Remove the cucumber from the liquid, and serve in a fresh bowl.

MARINATED ASPARAGUS

Asparagus is native to China, but until recently, it was used by the Chinese as a drug rather than a vegetable. This recipe, which uses typical Asian ingredients, makes a marvellous first course, regardless of whether it is of Chinese or Western origin.

You may feel there is not a great deal of sauce but it is enough to subtly and seductively flavour the asparagus. Too much, and it would overwhelm.

1 kg (2 lb) asparagus	1 tsp sesame oil
1 clove crushed garlic	3 tbsp peanut oil
1 tsp ginger juice	1 tbsp lemon juice
2 tsp soy sauce	pepper

Cut any tough woody ends from the asparagus and peel the stalk up to about the second point below the tips. Cook in a little salted water or steam until tender but still slightly crisp. Drain. I don't refresh in cold water, although this helps them retain their colour, because I think it removes some of the flavour.

Mix all the remaining ingredients together and stir well. Taste. You can adjust with seasonings at this stage. Place asparagus in a bowl, and pour the mixture over it, through a sieve to filter out the garlic pieces. With your hands, gently turn the asparagus over, being careful not to bruise or break any pieces.

Let marinate for about 2–2½ hours. Don't leave it longer than 4 hours because the asparagus will begin to lose colour and will tend to give out liquid into the marinade.

Arrange in a bouquet on individual plates. You can add a 'bow' of blanched spring onion top at the base.

Serves 6

COLD NOODLES WITH CHICKEN AND SPICY SAUCE

This style of Asian noodle dish is a perfect one-course meal, or you can serve tiny portions as a first course. Set out a little dish of chili or chili oil on the table so anyone who likes a little extra spark on their palate can spice up the noodles.

boned and skinned chicken breasts, about 500 g (1 lb) altogether

1 slice ginger

1 clove garlic

185 g (6 oz) thin egg noodles

1 tbsp oil

1 cucumber

SAUCE

½ small chili, seeds removed and flesh finely chopped

2 tbsp peanut butter

3 tsp sugar

1 large clove garlic, cut into pieces

2 tbsp red wine vinegar

½ cup (4 fl oz) chicken stock

1 tbsp soy sauce

1 slice peeled ginger, about 1.5 cm (½ in.)

2 tsp sesame oil

¼ cup finely chopped spring onion, including some of the green part

Note that if you like dishes with plenty of sauce you can double this quantity.

Put the chicken breasts with ginger and garlic into a small saucepan. Add enough water to just cover and a little salt. Bring slowly to the boil, then put on a lid and turn off the heat. Let the chicken breasts rest in the liquid for 30 minutes. By this time, they will be cooked, and will be very moist and tender. However, if for some reason you feel the chicken is not done enough, just bring gently to the boil again and cook over the lowest possible heat for a couple more minutes.

Refrigerate in the liquid and, when cold, pull the chicken away in long thin shreds, but retain the water in which it was cooked. Pour this into a large saucepan, adding more water to ¾ fill the pan. When boiling add the egg noodles. Cook, stirring occasionally so they don't stick to the base. When just soft, drain. Put into a bowl, add the oil and stir and toss with your hands to prevent them sticking together.

Peel the cucumber, cut into halves lengthwise and scoop out the seeds with a spoon. Cut the halves across into pieces of about 5 cm (2 in.), and then cut these pieces into strips. Chill the cucumber, covered.

Mix all the ingredients for the sauce in a blender and purée. It can be done hours in advance.

Near dinnertime put half the sauce over the noodles and toss. Spoon them onto a platter. Top with chicken shreds, more sauce, and cucumber strips. Finally, scatter chopped spring onions over the top.

Serves 4

STEAMED FISH

Never use filleted fish for Chinese dishes like this; the bones add flavour and keep the fish sweet and moist and, of course, hold the flesh together. Filleted fish tends to fall to bits in the steamer. Unless you have a really big steamer it is probably better to buy small whole fish, serving one per person, or perhaps one fish could be shared by two people.

Such fish as bream, baby snapper, and mullet are suitable for this dish. Thin, fine-textured fish like, for example, whiting could be used, but watch carefully because they could easily become overcooked.

4 small whole fish	*1 tbsp soy sauce*
3 Chinese mushrooms	*1 tbsp rice wine vinegar*
4 slices ginger, cut into thin shreds	*1 tsp sugar*
4 spring onions, cut into thin slices	*2 tsp oil*

Scale the fish, rinse and pat dry. Make a couple of deep slashes on each side of the thickest part of the fish, near the head.

Soak the Chinese mushrooms in warm water for about 30 minutes or until soft. Remove the tough stalks and cut the cap into thin slices.

Put a few bits of mushroom, ginger and spring onion on plates for the steamer, and put a fish on top.

Mix the remaining ingredients, and scatter over the fish. Steam for about 15 minutes, or according to the thickness of the fish. (It should flake easily, but be careful not to overcook.) Serve with the juices.

Serves 4

CHICKEN IN HOISIN SAUCE

This multi-coloured dish is usually served with roasted cashew nuts on top or on the side, so they will remain crisp. The nuts can be left out, although they do add to the dish. According to popular legend, the crown prince of China was travelling incognito around the country when he was served Chicken in Hoisin Sauce in a small restaurant in Shanghai. He was so enchanted by the flavours in the dish he stopped his tour, and immediately returned to Peking so he could relate the recipe to the imperial chef.

---

500 g (1 lb) chicken breast, boned and skinned

1 tsp sugar

2 tsp dry sherry, white wine or dry vermouth

1 tbsp oyster sauce

2 tsp sesame oil

1 tsp soy sauce

some black pepper

2 tbsp oil

1 red capsicum, seeded and cut into thin strips

2 stalks celery, cut into diagonal pieces

125 g (4 oz) small green beans, topped and tailed

$1/3$ cup water chestnuts, sliced or diced

1 clove garlic, finely chopped

1 tsp green ginger shreds

1 tbsp hoisin sauce

2 tbsp water

½ cup roasted cashew nuts (optional)

Cut the chicken into pieces about 2.5 cm (1 in.) square. Mix the sugar with sherry, oyster sauce, oil, soy and pepper, and pour over the chicken. Stir well, leaving to marinate for about 20 minutes.

Heat half the oil in a wok, add the capsicum, celery, beans and water chestnuts, and cook over high heat for a couple of minutes. Remove from the wok.

Heat the remaining tablespoon of oil, and add the garlic and ginger. Stir for 30 seconds and add the hoisin sauce and water. Put the chicken into this, pressing down gently so you have an even layer. When it has changed colour underneath, turn over and cook another minute or until the second side is sealed.

Return the vegetables to the pan and stir-fry until they are heated through, and the chicken is cooked. This should only take a minute or two.

Serves 4 (as part of multi-course meal)

LIGHT LEMON CHICKEN

In most versions of lemon chicken served in Western Chinese restaurants, this is a tart-sweet dish in which the chicken is fried in batter, then covered with a sticky lemon glaze. This recipe, however, is a totally different concept. I have adapted it from a recipe by American-Chinese author, Eileen Yin-Fei Lo, in her *Chinese Banquet Book*. It is fresh, tasting tart rather than sweet, and very light. I find it best to use thin-skinned lemon rather than thick, because the white pith adds bitterness.

1 chicken about 1.5 kg (3 lb)	2 tsp sesame oil
1½ lemons	2 tbsp chicken stock
1 tsp grated ginger	1 tbsp cornflour (cornstarch)
1 tbsp soy sauce	coriander pieces, finely chopped
1 tsp salt	spring onion tops or parsley (for
3 tsp sugar	garnish)
plenty of black pepper	

Cut the chicken into halves, then remove the wings and legs, and chop up into very small portions, bones and all. Rinse to make sure there are no bits of bone left, and pat dry.

Put into a shallow ovenproof dish or bowl which will fit into a steamer, and squeeze the juice of one lemon over the top. Cut the lemon half into a few thick slices and tuck these between the chicken pieces.

Mix all the remaining ingredients, except for cornflour and garnish. Pour them over the top of the chicken. Let stand to marinate for about 1 hour. Turn over once during this time.

Then steam, covered with foil or paper, over a medium heat for about 30–45 minutes. (Timing will depend on the size of your chicken pieces.)

Mix the cornflour with water. Tip the juices from the chicken into this and cook in a small pan, stirring constantly until lightly thickened.

Arrange the chicken in a bowl, pour sauce over the top and then scatter with the coriander, spring onion tops or parsley.

Serves 4

BEEF WITH A SPICED RICE POWDER

Don't be deterred by the rice powder preparation. It only takes a short time to make and lends a special flavour to the meat. You can buy it in some Asian shops, but the home-made version is better.

500 g (1 lb) rump or grilling steak, without any fat

MARINADE

2 tbsp soy sauce

2 tbsp rice wine

3 cloves roughly chopped garlic

2 tsp sesame oil

1 tbsp peeled, roughly chopped

fresh ginger

1 tbsp sugar

1 tsp chopped fresh chili,

   without any seeds

1 cup glutinous rice

1 tsp five-spice powder

¼ cup roughly-sliced spring
  onion

¼ tsp black pepper

finely-sliced spring onion

Cut the beef into strips 5 cm (2 in.) long and approximately 1.5 cm (1¼ in.) wide.

Put all the marinade ingredients into the blender and purée. Pour over the beef strips, stirring with your hands, and leave to marinate for any time between 1 hour and up to 12 hours.

Put the rice into a bowl, cover with hot water, let stand for 4 hours, and drain well. Then spread out on some kitchen paper to dry as much as possible.

Put the rice into a dry frying pan and cook, stirring every so often in the beginning, and constantly once it begins to dry. Cook until a golden to pale brown colour, and quite dry.

Remove and process to a powder, then mix with five-spice powder and pepper. It can be stored in a screw-top jar, in the refrigerator for weeks. Put some of the rice powder out on a plate or on some greaseproof paper.

Pick up the pieces of beef, gently shaking the marinade from them, and dip into the rice powder to coat. Put onto a clean plate. Once this is done, cook within a couple of hours.

Put the beef on a plate which will fit into a steamer. Cover with baking paper or foil and steam over a high heat for about 10 minutes.

Remove to a serving platter and scatter the top with spring onion. Any juices from the meat could be spooned over the rice.

Serves 4 (as part of multi-course meal)

STIR-FRIED BROCCOLI

Broccoli is a symbol of youth and good health to the Chinese, and its colour is a reminder of jade. It is a good source of vitamins and a wonderful vegetable when lightly cooked, so it is still crunchy.

375 g (12 oz) broccoli	2 tsp fresh ginger shreds
1 tbsp oil	¼ cup (2 fl oz) chicken stock or water
1 clove garlic, finely chopped	salt and pepper to taste

Chop the broccoli florets from the stalks. Peel the stalks and cut into strips. Heat the oil in a wok or large frying pan and add garlic and ginger. Fry until aromatic, tossing constantly.

Add the broccoli (florets and stalks) and stir-fry, tossing and turning for a minute. Tip the stock around the sides of the wok to create steam.

As soon as the broccoli is just barely tender, remove and serve immediately.

Serves 4

STIR-FRY OF BEEF AND TOMATOES

This is a tasty and easy family-style dish. Peking has a large supply of tomatoes in the summer months, and so this kind of dish is very popular.

500 g (1 lb) good quality grilling beef, e.g. fillet or rump steak

2 tbsp cornflour (cornstarch)

1 large egg white

2 tbsp oil

1 large onion, cut into halves and then thin slices

2 tsp shredded ginger

1 large clove garlic, finely chopped

2 tbsp water

4 diced tomatoes (about 500 g/1 lb)

1 tbsp soy sauce

Remove any fat from the meat and cut it into thin slices across. If these are thick, cut across again so you have strips about 5 cm by 2.5 cm. Mix the cornflour with egg white and add the meat. Mix with your hands so the meat is coated, and separate it.

Heat half the oil in a wok or frying pan and add the beef, just a few bits at a time, and stir-fry. Remove as each piece browns, then add more.

When all the meat is browned, add the remaining tablespoon of oil and heat. Add the onion, ginger and garlic and fry quickly, tossing until slightly limp.

Mix in water and tomatoes and fry gently about 5 minutes until you have plenty of lovely tomato juice.

Add the soy, return the beef pieces, and cook gently for a couple of minutes or until tender. Be careful not to overcook the meat.

Serves 4 (as part of multi-course meal)

BEEF SATE

This has no relation to the Malaysian dish which has tiny strips of beef on skewers. It is, however, a Singapore-style dish, which is often served in Canton.

This version is very popular as a home-cooked dinner. The spicy honey on the meat cooks to a wonderful brown coating. Serve it with rice, or you could simply provide a big mixed salad alongside it in a Western-style dinner. Be cautious with the honey you use. Some of the loveliest honey is great on bread but a bit rich or flowery for a marinade. If in doubt, add half the quantity and then add a little more to taste.

3 tbsp soy sauce	2 tbsp water
1 tbsp curry powder	4 thick pieces fillet or rump steak
¼ tsp cracked black pepper	an additional ¼ cup (2 fl oz)
2 tbsp honey	water

Mix the soy with curry, pepper, honey and water and stir well. Trim the meat of all fat and flatten the fillet steak lightly.

Pour the marinade into a shallow glass or china bowl and dip the meat into this, so both sides are coated. Place in one layer on a plate, and let marinate for about 4 hours.

Brush a flat tray with just a little oil and put the steaks on top. Have your griller (broiler) very hot and grill about 2 minutes on the first side before turning over and cooking for about a minute on the second side. Timing will of course vary according to your griller, the thickness of the steak, and how pink you like your meat. But be careful not to overcook.

While the steak is cooking tip any remaining liquid or marinade on the plate into a saucepan with the additional ¼ cup of water, and boil very hard for a minute until reduced slightly. Serve a little of this over the steak and rice. The steak can be presented whole or thinly sliced.

Serves 4

BARBECUED PORK

This very flavoursome preparation of pork, known as Char Sui, can be served as an appetiser or diced and added to a stir-fry, cut into tiny pieces for fried rice, or just eaten warm, sliced on the diagonal and accompanied by some rice.

The barbecued pork which you can buy in Asian shops is usually a highly-coloured red on the outside, and the texture almost chewy. The home-cooked version is not as vivid, but the flavour is as good if not better, and the meat is moist and tender.

It can be eaten warm or kept refrigerated and wrapped for about 4 days.

500 g (1 lb) pork fillet, any fat or sinew removed	*1 tbsp hoisin sauce*
¼ tsp salt	*½ tsp fresh ginger grated*
3 cloves garlic, crushed	*¼ tsp 5 spice powder*
1 tbsp soy sauce	*1 tbsp honey*
	1½ tbsp rice wine

If the pork is thick through, cut lengthwise to make several long strips from each fillet. Put into a bowl or shallow dish. Mix all the remaining ingredients and pour over the top. Leave to marinate 4 to 6 hours.

Put a little water in the base of a baking tin. Place a rack over this, and place the pork on top. Roast in a moderately-hot oven (200°C/450°F) for 20 minutes.

Brush with marinade on both sides and cook another 20 minutes or until well glazed and lightly speckled with brown.

Serves 4 (as part of multi-course meal)

ANTS CLIMBING TREES
(OR MINCED PORK WITH NOODLES)

In this strangely-named Chinese dish, the ants are the little pieces of pork, and the noodles are the branches of a twisted tree.

It may require a little imagination to visualise this, but it is a very tasty and easy dish. This is my version of it:

375 g (12 oz) finely-minced lean pork

2 tsp sugar

1 tbsp soy sauce

½ tsp finely chopped chili

1 tsp cornflour

125 g (4 oz) transparent noodles

1 tbsp oil

1 diced white onion

2 tbsp finely diced spring onion

1 tbsp fresh ginger shreds

1 tsp finely chopped chili

½ cup chicken stock (4 fl oz)

additional spring onion, finely
*   chopped or a few coriander*
*   leaves, plucked from the stems*
*   (for garnish)*

Mix the sugar, soy, chili and cornflour in a basin. Add the pork and stir well to mix through the meat. Leave to stand for about 30 minutes.

Put the transparent noodles into another bowl, pour hot water over the top and let stand about 25–30 minutes to soften. Drain.

Heat the oil, add the onion and cook, tossing for a couple of minutes. Add the spring onion and ginger with the chili and cook for another minute.

Now add the pork, stirring constantly until it has changed colour, and breaking it up so it doesn't pack into large pieces. Mix in the noodles and stock, and cook a few minutes until the pork is tender and the liquid has nearly all cooked away.

Mix in the spring onion and serve immediately, or scatter some coriander over the top when serving.

Serves 4

INDIA

To most people, Indian cooking means curry, spices and fiery food.
Yet this is not a true picture. Spices dominate Indian cuisine, curry
being just an overused word which, in theory, means little. The food
is flavoured by a blend of these spices, and may be hot, but can also
be mild. There is great delicacy in the flavours of some Indian
specialities, without any heat, in some regions. It is a cuisine of great
diversity.

Religion has played a big part in the development of eating; rules
and values dictating which foods cannot be touched according to caste
and religion. Because so many Indians are vegetarians, whether for
religious or economic reasons, there is an enormous variety of
vegetable dishes.

SPICY CHICK PEAS

This is a traditional snack dish which can be very gently reheated the next day over low heat. Serve in a bowl with quartered ripe tomatoes around the edge, some raw onion and, if you can cope with really hot tastes, some slivers of red chili.

250 g (8 oz) chick peas

½ tsp cumin seeds

2 tbsp oil

1 medium-sized onion, finely chopped

½ small chili, seeds removed and flesh chopped

1 tsp ground coriander

½ tsp salt

1 tsp mango powder

2 tsp grated fresh ginger

2 cloves crushed garlic

2 tbsp lemon juice

¼ cup coriander leaves (Chinese parsley)

Put the chick peas into a large bowl and cover with plenty of water, as they will swell and absorb it. Let soak 12 hours.

Simmer for about 1 hour, skimming the top when it first comes to the boil. Watch as it tends to froth and boil over. When tender, drain — but keep the water, as you need some of this to cook them again later.

Heat the oil and add cumin seeds, and cook for a minute or until aromatic, but don't let them darken. Grind them. If you don't have a pestle and mortar you can use the end of a rolling pin to crush them.

Return to the oil with all remaining ingredients, except the lemon juice and coriander. Cook a couple of minutes.

Add the chick peas and 1 cup (8 fl oz) of the liquid in which they were cooked. Simmer gently for about 15 minutes, stirring them occasionally, but being careful not to break up the peas.

Mix in the lemon and coriander. But if you intend to reheat this dish, add the lemon only, leaving the coriander until the day it is to be served, for a fresher taste.

Note: You can buy chick peas in tins and, although the flavour is not quite the same, these could be used for a quicker version of the dish. They would need cooking very gently for 15 minutes with the spices and some water to give them flavour. Stir carefully as these are more likely to break.

VEGETABLE PILAF

2 cups basmati or a long grain rice

1/3 cup unsalted cashew nuts

1 tbsp oil

1 onion, finely chopped

1 red pepper (minus seeds), finely diced

1.5 cm (¾ in.) piece ginger, peeled and cut into fine strips

1 clove garlic, finely chopped or crushed

2 small carrots, peeled and diced

125 g (4 oz) baby beans, cut into 4 cm (1½ in.) lengths

½ cup shelled peas

1 medium-sized eggplant, peeled and flesh cut into neat dice

4 cups (32 fl oz) water

1 tsp salt or to taste

¼ cup coriander (Chinese parsley) leaves

Wash the rice well and leave to drain thoroughly in a sieve.

Toast the cashew nuts in the oven, turning them over with a spatula a couple of times until they are toasted. Be careful they don't burn.

Heat the oil in a heavy-based saucepan and add onion, pepper, ginger and garlic. Cook gently for a few minutes, stirring until slightly softened.

Add the rice and stir-fry a couple of minutes. Mix in all the vegetables and water. Season. Bring to the boil, and cover the pan.

Cook without lifting the lid for 20 minutes. The rice and vegetables will be tender, and the water will be absorbed. Mound on a plate, scatter with the nuts and coriander leaves, and serve.

Serves 4–6

VEGETABLES IN GINGER

It's best if you can buy tiny vegetables for this: small white young cauliflower, tiny new potatoes and spring peas. Eaten with plain rice, it can make a lovely light meal.

1 tbsp oil	12 baby potatoes
¼ cup fresh ginger, peeled and cut into tiny matchstick pieces	1 cup fresh peas
	6 pea pods
2 cloves garlic, finely chopped	1 cup water (8 fl oz)
½ small cauliflower broken into tiny florets, the stalk sliced	salt to taste
	a small handful of coriander
1 tsp turmeric	(Chinese parsley leaves)

Heat the oil in a saucepan and add the ginger and garlic. Cook very gently, stirring for a couple of minutes until they are slightly softened.

Mix in the cauliflower and turmeric and stir until it is coated with gold. Add potatoes, peas and pods, water and salt. Bring to the boil, cover and simmer gently until the vegetables are quite tender but not mushy.

Remove the lid and boil for a couple of minutes until some of the liquid has reduced. (If you are concerned the vegetables will overcook, you could tilt the pan to remove the liquid and boil it separately for a few minutes, then return to the vegetables.)

Serve on a plate with the coriander leaves scattered on top.

Serves 4–6

DHAL

Lentils or pulses — known as dhals — are eaten daily in some form or another in most Indian homes. They are cheap and a high source of protein.

Used to accompany rice, either alongside or spooned over the top, it is also often served with Indian bread. Dahl is a dish which can be boring — unless it has a bit of spice on top to spark up the flavours. Fried onions or ginger, some roasted cumin seeds or whole mustard seeds or just a scatter of fresh coriander can provide this 'spark'.

One of the expressions used in northern India is, 'Dey dal may pani' ('Put water in the dahl') which refers to stretching food to serve more people by adding water. You sometimes find dhal served as a rather watery mixture but as a rule it is a soupy kind of dish. Dahl should be thinner than porridge but with more texture than pea soup.

I use arhar (often labelled toovar) dahl, a dull yellow grain, hulled and split, and the main dahl in southern India, for this dish.

1½ cups toovah dahl	1 tsp whole cumin seeds
2 small dried chili	1 tsp garam masala
2 whole cloves garlic	2 ripe tomatoes, diced small
2 thick sliced peeled ginger	some lemon wedges
1 tsp turmeric	garnish of mint or fresh coriander
2 tbsp oil	

Wash the dahl well. Put into a saucepan and add water to come about 2.5 cm (1 in.) over the top. Bring to the boil and remove the scum and froth that rises to the surface.

Add the chili, garlic, ginger and turmeric. Partly cover, leaving the lid a little ajar to let some steam escape. Simmer about 1 hour or until tender.

Prepare the topping when the dahl is almost ready. Heat the oil and add cumin seeds, letting them cook until aromatic. Stir. Add garam marsala and tomatoes, and toss over the heat for a couple of minutes.

If the dahl is too wet remove the lid, and boil the liquid quickly. Put the mixture into a shallow bowl, scatter the top with the tomato mixture and then some mint or coriander. Serve the lemon wedges around.

TANDOORI CHICKEN

One of the most familiar and publicised of all Indian dishes, the name 'tandoori' is from the clay oven (tandoor) in which it is cooked. The oven is usually buried in the ground and the chicken, threaded on a long skewer, lowered into the centre where it cooks over hot coals.

Until recent times this method of cooking was unknown in Delhi. It came from the north-west frontier. After the division of the Indian subcontinent streams of refugees crossed the border in the late 1940s, and one of these families opened a restaurant in an unfashionable part of Delhi.

Called the Pearl Palace, it was very plain and simple, serving meat, fish, chicken or bread cooked in the tandoor. At first, locals frequented the restaurant, then well-known and wealthy families began to eat there. It is considered a landmark in Delhi, all kinds of people wending their way to try the original tandoor.

The meat is marinated first, turning a bright orange-red colour from vegetable dye. This makes it look rather dry, but it has a moist texture and a marvellous flavour.

I skip the dye and use instead a little paprika to give some colour, although it is nowhere near as bright as the traditional version. This simple variation, made with skim-milk yoghurt, while not the same, makes a delicious main course dish.

Lemon wedges are served with tandoori chicken, as are wafer-thin slices of onion, which have been left in ice water so they are mild and crisp.

1 chicken about 1.5 kg (3 lb) or	*2 large cloves garlic, crushed*
2 baby chickens	*1 tsp paprika*
1 tsp coriander seeds	*½ tsp (or to taste) chili powder*
1 tsp cumin seeds	*½ tsp salt*
2 tsp grated ginger	*1 cup (8 fl oz) low-fat yoghurt*

Cut the chickens into portions (if baby chickens, into halves). Remove all the skin. Once loosened, it will lift easily. Using a small sharp knife, cut some slashes diagonally on the breast, and several slits to the bone on the legs so the marinade will penetrate.

Put the coriander and cumin seeds into a dry frying pan and cook until they smell aromatic, stirring. Grind. Mix with the remaining ingredients. Put the chicken into a china basin or glass dish and pour the marinade over it, turning the chicken over, so all is coated. Cover and refrigerate for 24 hours.

Turn once or twice during the marinating period. Place some non-stick baking paper in a baking dish and lightly oil the top. Remove the chicken from the marinade and put into the pan, so there is a tiny space between the pieces. Bake in a moderate oven (180°C/350°F) for about 20 minutes, then baste with any juices, turn over and cook for a further 15 minutes, or until cooked through. Keep basting because, as there is no skin on the chicken, you need to keep it moist.

Serves 4–6

GRILLED CHICKEN BREAST

I have adapted this from one of Madhur Jaffrey's recipes in *Invitation to Indian Cooking*, using far less oil. This doesn't seem to affect the moist flavour. This light, spicy dish is wonderfully versatile because it can be served both hot and cold. Just be careful not to overcook the chicken or you will dry it out.

4 chicken breasts	¼ tsp cayenne pepper
1 tbsp oil	1 tsp salt
1 medium-sized onion, roughly diced	3 tbsp white wine vinegar
4 cloves garlic, chopped	4 cloves
2.5 cm piece fresh ginger, sliced thinly	1 tbsp tomato purée or ½
2 tsp ground coriander	tablespoon tomato paste
½ tsp cinnamon	¼ tsp cumin seeds

Remove skin from the chicken. Grind all the remaining ingredients in a blender. Cut each chicken breast into three long strips. Put them into a bowl, add the marinade and pat it all over the chicken breasts, so they are well covered on all sides. The mixture will be moist but thick. Cover and refrigerate for 3 hours. Remove 20 minutes before cooking so it is not too cold.

Oil a sheet of foil. Pre-heat the griller, and place the chicken pieces onto this. Put them under the griller and cook on the first side for about 5–6 minutes (depending on the thickness of the chicken breast and the heat of your griller), then about 3 minutes on the other side. Test if not sure it's cooked. A knife should go through easily, and the juices not be pink. Be careful not to overcook it or it will get too dry. If you prefer, it can be baked on foil in a moderate oven, (180°C/350°F) for about 15–18 minutes.   Serve with some salad.

Serves 4

KHEEMA

This is an easy family-style dish which is tasty and inexpensive. There are all kinds of kheema (which literally means 'minced'). It can be made with beef or lamb, yoghurt can be added, and it can be cooked with peas or potatoes. It also makes a good stuffing for such vegetables as tomato, eggplant or capsicum.

Just be sure to buy good-quality, lean meat. If you can't obtain this, cook the dish beforehand, let it cool and remove any fat from the top before reheating.

Serve with a dish of rice and a dish of relish, and you have a satisfying meal.

---

750 g (1½ lb) finely ground beef or
   lamb

4 cloves garlic

2 onions, roughly chopped

1 tbsp chopped ginger

3 tbsp water

1 tbsp oil

1 cinnamon stick

3 whole cloves

1 tsp ground black pepper

1 small red chili, seeds removed
   and chili sliced

1 tbsp coriander

1 tsp ground cumin

1 bay leaf

3 ripe tomatoes, roughly diced

4 medium-sized potatoes, cut into
   quarters

1 tsp salt or to taste

½ cup water

1 tbsp lemon juice

Put the garlic, onion, ginger and water into a blender and process until a purée.

Heat oil in a non-stick saucepan, add cinnamon, cloves, pepper, chili, coriander, cumin and bay leaf, and cook a minute, stirring the spices. Add the garlic and onion paste and cook about five minutes. Keep stirring.

Add meat, stir and turn to break up all the lumps and cook until it has changed colour and starts to brown.

Mix in tomatoes and potatoes and add the water and lemon. Cover and cook gently for about 45 minutes, or until the potatoes are quite tender. It will depend on the variety. Before serving be sure to remove the cinnamon stick.

Serves 4–6

STEAMED PRAWNS

Eastern India has a special bias towards the beautiful cooking of Bengal. The bright yellow fields of mustard seeds give the landscape its name, Golden Bengal, and provide an ingredient which is a vital part of Bengali fish cooking.

It is essential to use green, uncooked prawns. They can be cooked in a basin standing in a pan of hot water. When cooked, they will be tinged with gold — aromatic and surrounded with a little flavoursome prawn juice.

500 g (1 lb) large, green prawns,
shelled but tail left on
1 tsp turmeric
1 tsp yellow or black mustard seeds
¼ tsp salt

½ small red chili, seeds removed
1 tbsp oil
1 tsp fresh ginger, chopped finely
½ tsp sugar

Remove the back vein from the prawns. Put all the remaining ingredients into a blender and process until fine. Mix with the prawns, stirring with your hands so they are well coated. Put the prawns into a china basin, large enough for them to reach only two-thirds of the way up. Cover with foil and tie firmly.

Place this basin into a saucepan of hot water which comes halfway up the sides. Cook covered with a lid for about 15 minutes, adding more water if it boils away.

If the prawns are not ready, simply put the foil back on top and continue cooking — the timing may vary according to the basin, individual heat, etc.

Remove and serve them with rice, spooning remaining liquid in the bowl over the top.

Serves 4–6

CHAPATI

This is a simple bread which accompanies Indian dishes, and is broken off in pieces to scoop up the food and juices. I always imagined chapatis would be difficult to make, but find them quite simple. The flavour of wholewheat flour with the puffy texture and taste is both light and chewy at the same time. The most important thing is to be patient and knead it well; the more it is kneaded the lighter the dough.

2 cups wholemeal flour or 1½ cups	*½ tsp salt*
wholemeal flour and ½ cup white flour	*¾ cup water*

Put the flour with salt into a bowl. Gradually add the water and mix until the flour holds. As flours can vary, don't add it all until you are sure you need it. If the mixture is dry you may have to add more flour. (The mixture should hold together and be slightly sticky.)

Put out on a bench and knead for about 8–10 minutes. If too

sticky, scatter a little flour on the bench. Roll into a ball and cover with a damp cloth and leave to stand for 1–3 hours. If you want to keep it longer wrap in plastic-wrap and refrigerate for 24 hours. This will make it even lighter.

Knead a little again and divide into 16 pieces. While you roll one out, keep the remaining balls of dough under the damp cloth.

Flour a board lightly, flatten the dough and roll out evenly into a circle about 12.5 cm (5 in.) in diameter. As it can be sticky, keep dusting with flour.

Chapatis are cooked in a *tava* in India. I use a heavy-based frying pan which I find satisfactory, but it must be very hot. They are cooked with some ghee brushed over the base of the pan. You can use oil if you prefer not to use any butter, although butter is better for this particular dish. Cook the first chapatis you rolled, as the little resting time makes it lighter.

When the pan is smoking hot drop the chapati on it, and bubbles should form. It will take between 45 seconds to a minute. Turn over, using tongs, and cook on the other side. With a folded tea towel or an egg slice, press down on the edges to make them bubbly. As soon as it is cooked and has light brown spots on the sides, lift off. In India, chapatis are then picked up with tongs and held over a gas flame for a few seconds, and they puff up immediately.

As you cook each one, put inside a tea towel and continue cooking the remainder. Wrapped in some foil with the package edges firmly shut, they keep warm for about 30 minutes.

Although top Indian cooks would probably be horrified, if I can't manage to prepare them at the last moment, I do them in advance and gently warm through in the oven in some foil at dinnertime.

Makes about 16

TOMATO, ONION AND LEMON RELISH

This is a refreshing side dish which goes well with almost all Indian dishes. It can be served plain or with green sprigs of coriander scattered on top. Serve chilled.

1 large tomato

1 medium-sized mild white onion or odourless onion

½ tsp salt

1 tsp roasted cumin seeds, finely ground

pinch cayenne pepper

¼ tsp freshly ground black pepper

1 tbsp lemon or lime juice

Chop the tomato into small dice, leaving the skin on. This will hold the pieces in better shape and the relish won't become mushy when stored.

Dice the onion very finely and mix with the tomato, and then gently stir in the remaining ingredients. Taste. It should be fresh and tart — you can adjust with more lemon if needed.

Cover and chill several hours before serving. It can be kept for about 12 hours. (If very wet, you can drain this relish a little.)

CUCUMBER RAITA

'Raita' means a dish made with a vegetable and yoghurt. Cucumber raita has a refreshing, cooling effect in your mouth after spicy foods, and goes with almost all Indian dishes. Sometimes the cucumber is grated, and at other times, sliced. Personally, I prefer the slices of cucumber for their crisp texture. Remove the seeds first to prevent the cucumber becoming too watery.

A small amount of roasted cumin seeds is used. These can be done in a larger quantity and used as needed, storing the remainder in an airtight jar in the refrigerator.

1 large cucumber, peeled
1½ cups plain low-fat yoghurt
½ tsp salt
pinch cayenne pepper (optional)

½ tsp roasted cumin seeds
coriander (Chinese parsley) to
*   garnish*

Cut the cucumber into halves lengthwise and remove the seeds, using a teaspoon. Cut into very thin slices.

Stir all the remaining ingredients into the yoghurt and mix gently. Stir this into the cucumber slices, and refrigerate for about an hour. Use within 4–5 hours; it will gradually become wet the longer it stands.

Serve plain or with some chopped coriander on top.

MARINATED LAMB CHOPS

Northern Indian food is more aromatic than fiery hot, and lamb is an important meat in the region. (The Muslims won't eat pork, and the Hindus won't eat beef as they consider the cow a sacred animal.)

Any lamb chop is suitable for this dish. Use loin, chump or leg, but make sure you trim it well. The flavour of the meat mingles with the many spices, and it is moist and succulent. Serve with salad and a rice dish on the side.

8 lamb chops, all fat removed

1 cup low-fat yoghurt

½ tsp salt

1 tsp grated ginger

4 cloves crushed or finely-chopped garlic

1 tsp chili paste (or to taste)

¼ tsp garam marsala

1 tbsp poppy seeds, ground

Trim chops well, but don't cut them so much they fall to bits. Mix all remaining ingredients and add chops, stir around so they are coated on all sides with the mixture. Cover and refrigerate for 12 hours. Remove a couple of hours before cooking so they are at room temperature.

Put on a grilling tray under a pre-heated griller and cook (depending on their thickness.) about 5 minutes on the first side, and 3 minutes on the second side. Let rest one minute for the juices to settle, and serve with chilled, water-thin onion rings.

Serves 4

STEAMED FISH

Similar to the Bengali steamed prawn dish, the fish is placed in a basin with some spices and cooked gently until tender. It will be tinged with gold and very sweet and flavoursome. Most fish can be cooked by this method, but it is better to make sure the fish is boneless and not to use fine-textured fish, such as whiting, which can break too easily. Serve the fish and its juices with rice and a cucumber salad.

4 fillets fish
2 tsp mustard seeds
2 tsp turmeric
½ tsp salt

½ tsp cumin
¼ tsp chili paste, or half chili finely chopped

Cut the fish into pieces about 5 cm x 10 cm. Grind or crush the mustard seeds and mix with the remaining spices. Rub this mixture into the pieces of fish, using your fingers.

Put the fish into a wide-based basin in which it will fit so it comes only about two-thirds of the way up. Cover with foil and tie firmly around the edge. Put into a saucepan of hot water to come halfway up the sides of the basin and cook (covered) for about 15 minutes.

Turn off the heat and let the fish sit in the basin for 5 minutes, and then remove the foil. If it is not ready you can return and cook a little longer without spoiling it.

Be sure to spoon the juices from the bowl around the fish.

Serves 4

SPECIAL INGREDIENTS
The following ingredients play an important part in Indian cooking.

BASMATI RICE
An aromatic rice with a delicate flavour. It goes well with Western foods or can be eaten on its own. Best with more delicate dishes from northern India rather than fiery spiced food.

CORIANDER SEEDS
The main ingredient in commercial curry powder, those seeds are round and light brown. They are the dried seed of the coriander plant which is sometimes known as Chinese parsley.

CUMIN SEEDS (ROASTED)
These can be scattered over cooked vegetable dishes or snacks. If stored in a sealed jar in the refrigerator they will keep for a month, although the flavour decreases with time. It is worth roasting enough to fill a small jar, to keep on hand. They are used in both the accompaniment relishes in this chapter. Put about 4 tablespoons of seeds into a heavy-based pan over medium heat and cook, stirring constantly until they smell aromatic and roasted. Grind them or crush with a mortar and pestle.

GARAM MARSALA
A mix of cardamon, cinnamon, cloves, nutmeg, cumin and pepper, which is scattered or mixed through food at the end of the cooking time. It can be bought powdered in shops, but be sure it is fresh. You can grind your own mix. Add the spices to suit your own taste. My favourite recipe is 1 tablespoon cardamon seeds, a 2.5 cm stick (1 in.) cinnamon, and 1 teaspoon each of cumin seeds, whole cloves, black pepper, and nutmeg — ground together in a blender or coffee grinder until powdery. You will end up with about 3 tablespoons. Store in an airtight jar in a cool place away from light.

GHEE
Clarified butter which can be used for frying, without it burning. It has a slightly nutty flavour and can be bought, usually in cans, in some supermarkets and at almost all Asian food stores.

It is free of milk solids so in theory refrigeration is not needed, but I prefer to store it in the refrigerator or freezer. As this is a low-fat book, I have substituted oil in these recipes, and the flavour is naturally altered slightly. If you would like to cook the chapatis, for example, in a pan with ghee, the taste will be more authentic. The choice is yours.

MANGO POWDER
Made from dried unripe mango, this powder gives a tart, sour flavour to dishes.

MUSTARD SEEDS
Dark yellow in colour, these seeds are mild if left whole. They become hot when ground. Tiny and round mustard seeds jump and spit in the pan when cooked in oil, so don't leave them too long on the stove.

TOOVAH DAHL (OR TOOR DAHL)
One of the multitude of dahl, this is also known as arha dahl, the main dahl of Southern India. It is a hulled, dull yellow pea which you must wash well before using.

TURMERIC
Fresh with its spread 'fingers', it resembles a piece of ginger. A bright yellow colour, the powder is believed by some Indians to aid digestion. It imparts colour and just a small amount of flavour to food. Fresh turmeric is preferable.

SINGAPORE AND MALAYSIA

At the crossroads of Asia, Singapore is a whole world of culinary delight, combining the dishes of China, Malaysia, India and Europe. It was difficult to pick out individual dishes as so many similar ones have appeared in their own chapters in this book.

Instead, I have listed some 'hawker' dishes, the popular everyday food sold at roadside stalls and some, the Nonya food, which I consider uniquely Singaporean. This food was created over time by the Straits women, the most famous of all being the late Mrs Lee.

History tells of Chinese immigrants who came to Malaysia more than 400 years ago, and settled in Malacca. The men took on Malay wives and customs. Their language and food gradually blended. The cooking which developed has distinctive tastes and flavours.

Nonya food is time-consuming to prepare. It is heavily spiced and uses pungent roots such as turmeric and ginger, aromatic leaves, candlenuts, chilis and shrimp paste, and lime or green mangoes to add tart flavours. It is difficult to find in restaurants because of the preparation involved.

The most important domestic duty for the young Straits-born Chinese girls was to be a good cook, and their training in preparing Nonya food began early.

According to the late Mrs Lee, it takes many years of study to make Nonya dishes perfectly. With her words ringing in my ears, I have therefore chosen the simplest examples of Nonya food and of course fresh-tasting and low fat dishes.

Serve them all on the table as you would a Chinese meal, with rice to accompany them. Fruit is not eaten at the end of the meal. Instead cakes of glutinous rice and coconut milk are eaten, and coffee, not tea, is drunk.

MALAYSIAN BEEF STEW

In this dish, the beef is first marinated, giving the stew a rich flavour and good colour. It can be reheated most successfully. Although ingredients include potato, rice would traditionally accompany this dish. But if you prefer, you could simply serve it with a salad.

750 g (1½ lb) casserole-type beef
1 tsp ground black pepper
1 tbsp soy sauce
1 tbsp white vinegar
2 tbsp oil
2 onions, cut into thin slices
2 cloves garlic, crushed
2 tsp grated ginger

3 whole cloves
3 cardamon pods
1 cinnamon stick
1 cup (8 fl oz) water or beef stock
*2 medium-sized potatoes, peeled
and cut into small dice*
salt to taste

Remove any fat from the meat, and cut into pieces of about 2.5 cm (1 in.). Mix the pepper, soy and vinegar in a bowl, add the meat, and stir to coat. Let it marinate for about an hour.

Heat the oil in a saucepan, add the onion and cook gently over a low heat until soft. Add the garlic and ginger, and fry a few minutes, then mix in the beef, a handful at a time. Stir until it has browned. Remove it, and add more meat, browning it, until it has all been sealed.

Return all the meat, and add the spices, marinade and water or stock. Bring to the boil. Cover the pan and let it cook over a very low heat for about an hour, or until the meat is tender.

Add the potatoes and salt, and cook for a further 20 minutes, until the potatoes are just soft.

Before serving you can remove the cinnamon stick and cardamon pods or, if you wish, leave them in. They are not, of course, meant to be eaten.

Serves 6

CHICKEN SOUP WITH SMALL MACARONI

This simple Singaporean soup would be classified as a home-style dish. It's very tasty, provided you have some nicely-flavoured chicken stock, and can be served as soon as it is made, or reheated.

4 cups (32 fl oz) chicken stock	1/3 cup finely-chopped shallots
2 stalks celery, finely sliced	½ tsp black pepper
2 small chicken breasts, or one large	1 tsp sugar
1 tbsp oil	125 g (4 oz) small macaroni

Put the stock into a saucepan, and add celery. Bring to the boil, cook covered, for about 10 minutes, or until the celery is almost tender.

Remove the skin and bones from chicken breasts, and add. Heat the soup again and cook on the lowest heat for about 6 minutes. Turn off the heat and let the chicken sit for about another 10 minutes. It will be cooked but very moist.

Remove the chicken breasts with a fork or slotted spoon and, as soon as they are cool enough to handle, shred into strips or cut into dice. Return to the soup.

Heat the oil in a small pan, add shallots and cook until a golden-brown. Drain on some kitchen paper. Add pepper and sugar to the soup.

Cook the macaroni separately in a pot of salted water and drain. Add to the soup.

When ready to serve put a little of the golden fried shallots in each soup bowl, and pour boiling soup over the top. You can garnish with a little finely-chopped spring onion if you wish. It can be reheated but be careful not to overcook the chicken.

Serves 4

SPICY PRAWNS WITH LEMON

This quick and delicious dish from Malaysia is slightly sour and hot in flavour.

500 g (1 lb) raw prawns, peeled	*2 tbsp oil*
2 tbsp roughly-chopped shallots	*8 cashew nuts*
1 chili (minus seeds), roughly diced	*2 large tomatoes, cut into dice*
2 cloves garlic	*½ tsp salt*
3 tsp grated ginger	*3 tsp sugar*
1 tsp prawn paste	*2 tbsp lemon juice*

Remove the dark vein from the prawns. Into a food processor, place the shallots, chili, garlic, ginger, prawn paste, oil and cashew nuts (or you could blend the spices).

Put this mixture into a frying pan and cook, stirring until aromatic. Add the prawns and fry, turning until they have changed colour. Add tomatoes, salt, sugar and cook until the tomato has formed a sauce in the pan, and the prawns are ready.

The cooking time should be only about 3–4 minutes at the most. Mix in lemon juice, stir it through gently and taste for seasonings.

Serves 4

SINGAPORE-STYLE NOODLES

Noodle dishes are among the most famous of the Singapore 'hawker' dishes. They are served steaming hot, ladled into bowls with all kinds of savoury titbits. Ideal for a quick and easy lunch dish or party dish. Of course, you can vary the ingredients with whatever fresh vegetables are in season, or with the meat or fish of your choice.

500 g (1 lb) fresh yellow noodles	2 tbsp oil
8 raw prawns (shrimps)	2 cloves garlic, crushed
250 g (8 oz) pork, cut into very thin slices or finely diced	1 fresh red chili (minus seeds), diced small
2 cups chicken stock (16 fl oz)	2 stalks celery, cut into thin slices
2 tsp soy sauce	1 small onion, finely diced
1 tsp sugar	1½ cups fresh bean shoots
2 eggs	

GARNISH

finely chopped spring onion	leaves of coriander
a little red chili	

Put the noodles into a bowl, pour boiling water over the top to soften, and separate. Drain.

Cut prawns into halves. Put the pork into a saucepan with stock, soy and sugar and simmer very gently until the meat is tender. This should take only about 15 minutes.

Beat the egg. Brush a pan with a little oil or use a non-stick pan. When hot add sufficient egg to coat the base with a thin layer and cook until set. Let rest a minute, turn out and repeat process until all the egg has been cooked. When cold, roll up the omelettes and cut into thin strips.

Heat the oil in a wok or large frying pan, and add garlic, chili, celery and onion, and fry until aromatic.

Add the pork and prawns and toss until the prawns have changed colour. Mix in bean shoots and noodles along with about ¾ cup of the chicken stock in which you cooked the pork. Toss until everything is very hot and well mixed.

Serve in bowls or on a large platter topped with spring onion, chili, coriander leaves and omelette strips.

Serves 4

CHICKEN WITH SOY AND LEMON

A Nonya dish, very easy to make, with a deep colour and interesting, slightly salty, sweet flavour.

1 chicken, 1.5 kg (3 lb)	1 tbsp sugar
1 tbsp oil	2 tbsp soy
2 onions, cut into halves and thinly sliced	½ cup (4 fl oz) water
	1 tbsp lemon juice
1 chili (minus seeds), finely diced	

Heat oil in a saucepan. Add the onion and chili, and cook a few minutes, or until the onion has slightly wilted.

Cut the chicken into small portions. Add these and cook, turning the pieces over until they have changed colour.

Add all the remaining ingredients and cook very gently over low heat, turning the chicken over several times until it is tender and the sauce is reduced to a very small amount of juice.

Lastly add the lemon juice and mix it through before serving.

Serves 4

CHICKEN CURRY CAPTAIN

A rather mild Malaysian curry. The name supposedly originated when a captain asked a Chinese cook what was for dinner that night. 'Curry, Captain', was the reply, and this is what he served.

There are a number of variations; some use coconut milk which, although delicious, is high in fat. For this reason, I am giving the version without the coconut milk.

1 chicken, 1.5 kg (3 lb) or equivalent in chicken portions	2 tbsp oil
	3 large onions, cut into thin slices
2 large cloves garlic, crushed	1 small red chili (minus seeds), finely sliced
1 tsp ground turmeric	
1 tsp ground salt	¾ cup (6 fl oz) water
½ tsp ground black pepper	½ lemon

If using a whole chicken, cut into portions, and pat the chicken pieces dry. Mix the garlic with turmeric, salt and pepper. Rub this paste into the chicken and let it stand about 20 minutes.

Heat oil in a saucepan, add one of the sliced onions and fry gently until golden-brown. Remove and drain on kitchen paper. Add the remaining onion with chili and fry until golden.

Then add chicken pieces, turn up the heat and cook until the chicken has changed colour. Add water, bring to the boil, and simmer, covered, until the chicken is almost tender. Remove the lid and continue cooking, turning the chicken over from time to time until it is tender and the liquid has almost evaporated.

Serve with reserved onion on top and squeeze on the lemon juice. Accompany with a rice or potato dish.

Serves 4

SALAD JAVA

This is a salad which could be served as part of a multi-course meal. It is slightly spicy, deliciously fresh-tasting, and keeps well for 24 hours.

1 long continental cucumber, or	*2 cups diced fresh pineapple*
2 small cucumbers	

DRESSING

1 small red chili (minus seeds), diced	*2 tbsp sugar*
	2 tbsp vinegar
1 tbsp fish paste	*2 tbsp water*

Peel the cucumber, and cut into halves lengthwise. Scoop out the seeds and cut the cucumber into small short strips, or neat dice. Mix with the pineapple dice in a bowl.

Pound the chili and mix with the remaining ingredients. Pour over the cucumber and pineapple and stir to coat.

Chill, covered, for about an hour to let the flavours blend before serving.

Serves 6 as an accompaniment

PORK IN TAMARIND SAUCE

A Nonya dish, this combines a sharp tamarind mixture with the heat of chili and a little sugar, so it is not too sour. The juices will cook away slightly and the dark sauce should just be sufficient to coat the meat. It can be reheated gently, if you wish to make it in advance.

500 g (1 lb) fat-free pork	*1 tsp dried shrimp paste*
2 tbsp tamarind	*1 tbsp oil*
¾ cup (6 fl oz) hot water	*½ tsp salt*
1 medium-sized onion, finely diced	*2 tsp sugar*
1 red chili (minus seeds), diced small	

Cut the pork into dice about 2.5 cm (1 in.). Put the tamarind into a small bowl, add water, and leave to soak for 10 minutes. Squeeze with your fingers, and then pour through a sieve into a bowl.

Mix onion with the chili and shrimp paste. Heat the oil in a saucepan, add the onion mixture and fry, stirring until aromatic.

Add the pork and stir until it has changed colour, then mix in the tamarind water, salt and sugar. Bring to the boil, then turn the heat down very low and cook, stirring occasionally until the pork is tender and sauce reduced. This usually takes about 45 minutes, but will depend on the quality of the pork.

Serve with rice.

Serves 4

FISH IN TAMARIND SAUCE

A Malay dish, this is called Garam Assam. The word 'Garam' means 'to be irresistible'. This particular dish is supposed to stimulate the appetite with its interesting fresh, slightly sour, flavour. It could be made with fish fillets, but I find it nicest of all with whole fish, such as baby snapper, on the bone. The flesh is even sweeter and the fish won't break up in the sauce, as can happen with fillets.

2 whole fish or 4 fillets of fish	*5 candlenuts*
2 tbsp tamarind	*2 tbsp finely chopped shallots*
1 cup (8 fl oz) hot water	*2 cloves garlic*
8 baby Japanese long eggplant or	*1 tbsp shrimp paste*
250 g (8 oz) round eggplant	*1 tbsp oil*
2 slices fresh ginger	*2 tsp sugar*
1 tsp black pepper	*½ tsp salt*
½ tsp turmeric	

Mix tamarind with hot water, work with your fingers and strain, discarding the tamarind.

Peel the eggplant. Cut the baby ones into halves, the larger round eggplant into large dice or wedges. Salt lightly, and let stand for 30 minutes before rinsing, then pat dry.

Put the ginger, pepper, turmeric, candlenuts, shallots, garlic and shrimp paste into a food processor, and purée to a paste.

Heat a frying pan, add the oil, and stir-fry the spice paste. Scatter about ¼ cup tamarind water over the top and continue to stir-fry.

Add eggplant and remaining tamarind water, sugar and salt. Cook gently until the eggplant has slightly softened, and then add the fish.

Cover the pan and cook for about 5 minutes. Turn the fish over very carefully and replace the lid on the pan and continue to cook gently, until the fish is tender. This will take about 10–12 minutes for a whole fish, and only about 5–6 minutes for thinner fish fillets.

Serves 4

PORK AND RICE VERMICELLI

A simple home-style Nonya dish which can be served with rice and a green salad.

½ cup fine vermicelli	1 tbsp soy sauce
2 tbsp oil	¹/₃ cup water (2½ fl oz)
2 large potatoes (about 375 g/	plenty of freshly cracked black
12 oz), cut into very	pepper
small dice	salt
2 onions, thinly sliced	1 tsp sugar
375 g (12 oz) finely-minced lean	an additional ¼ cup (2 fl oz)
pork	water

Put the vermicelli into a bowl and cover with hot water, then leave to soak while you cook this dish.

Heat the oil in a saucepan, add the potatoes and cook until golden, turning them every so often. Add the onions and cook a few minutes, then add the pork, stirring constantly until it has changed colour.

Drain the vermicelli and add with the soy, water, pepper, salt and sugar, and cook over low heat for about 5 minutes. Add the remaining water, and return to the boil. It is now ready to serve.

Serves 4

KOREA

If you were to glance through any Korean home, whether it was the humblest room or a modern apartment, you would find one thing in common. Tucked away in a corner, on an outside balcony, or in the yard there would be a number of jars holding the pickles and spices which form a major part of Korean cooking.

They accompany every meal, even breakfast, the most important of the pickles being kimchee. Based on a Korean cabbage which is stuffed with chili, onion, ginger and radish, it is left to ferment. The cabbage becomes sour and hot and adds spice to the simplest dish.

When researching Korean food I found sesame seeds or sesame oil seemed to be included in or scattered over almost every dish, adding a wonderfully nutty and delicious flavour. Korean food is very hot, the spiciness coming from fresh or dried chili or a red, rather lethal chili powder. From an early age, children are gradually introduced to spicy foods until they develop a taste for them.

Because most Western palates are not adjusted to very hot chili, I have used less in these recipes, giving a gentle taste of heat rather than an overwhelming blast. However, of course, quantities can be adjusted to suit individual tastes.

Everyday Korean food is quite simple. Rice is served with every meal, accompanied by a fish or vegetable dish and, of course, kimchee. The rice is a slightly sticky variety, similar to that of Japan.

Pork and chicken are also used in Korean cooking. The country now has more than 2 million head of cattle, and beef, once very expensive, is now more readily available for local consumption.

One of the best Korean dishes is a marinated beef, 'bulgogi' a fat-free, highly-flavoured, utterly delicious meat dish. Lamb is never eaten, yet imaginative combinations of meat and fish (from the sea which surrounds three sides of the Korean peninsula) are popular. You may find stew, for example, with both fish and beef.

Korean food hasn't achieved world acclaim, the best-known dish probably being their 'steam boat'. This has a central chimney surrounded by a moat which holds the food. The chimney is filled with hot coals and food is cooked in a simmering stock around it. It is one dish which I haven't included, as it involves buying special equipment. I have tried to avoid this when other simpler dishes are equally good.

BEAN SHOOT SALAD

This is served on the table as a side dish. It is so light, fresh-tasting and nutritious that it needn't be reserved for Korean meals. It could be part of any salad buffet or dinner.

6 spring onions, cut into 3-cm lengths

3 cups bean shoots

SAUCE

2 tbsp toasted sesame seeds

¼ cup (2 fl oz) light soy sauce

1 tbsp rice wine vinegar

1½ tsp sugar

1 chili (minus seeds), finely chopped

1 clove crushed garlic

1 tsp sesame oil

a little salt to taste, if you wish

Half-fill a medium-sized saucepan with water, and bring to the boil. Add the bean shoots, count to five, then drain them. Rinse with cold water. Drain well, mix with spring onions, and chill.

Grind the sesame seeds and mix with all the remaining ingredients. Refrigerate if not using immediately.

At dinnertime mix the sauce with the bean shoots and spring onions and toss well. Serve immediately. If kept for too long the bean shoots begin to soften in the liquid and are not as fresh tasting.

KIMCHEE

Throughout autumn, when cabbage is very sweet, the large Chinese cabbage is sold in huge quantities to make kimchee. According to a kimchee museum in Seoul, there are 160 varieties, made from all kinds of vegetables.

The cabbage kimchee is the main pickle, and this has many variations. Some are quite complex and require lengthy periods to bubble away and ferment, developing a typical sour, hot flavour. In country areas, large vats of kimchee are buried in the ground so it won't freeze.

This version is an easy one, a short-cut method which gives a very tasty pickle. It won't keep indefinitely (as will the kimchee made by traditional methods) but makes a tasty accompaniment to Korean dishes.

1 medium-sized Chinese cabbage
3 tbsp coarse or sea salt
5 cups (40 fl oz) water
6 finely-chopped spring onions
6 finely-chopped cloves garlic

2 tsp chili powder
1 tbsp grated fresh ginger
¼ cup white wine vinegar
sesame oil

Cut the cabbage into halves lengthwise, and then into coarse slices. Now cut across again, so you have rough pieces. Rinse well.

Mix the salt and water in a large bowl and add the cabbage. Put a plate on top to weight the cabbage down, so it won't bob above the water. Leave to stand for 8 hours. Knead it with your hands and then drain and rinse again. Drain well. Mix all the remaining ingredients, except for the sesame oil, and add to the cabbage.

Put into a large glass jar or earthenware container and let stand for 24 hours.

Refrigerate. It will keep for about a week to 10 days. Before serving, scatter a little sesame oil over the top.

BULGOGI

Meats of all kinds can be cooked in this Korean barbecue style. Originally, the meat was grilled on iron hotplates. Nowadays it is cooked at the table on cone-shaped hotplates, specially designed to fit over tabletop burners.

At home, you can either use a barbecue, or cook the meat in a heavy-based pan or under a pre-heated griller (broiler). It cooks almost immediately and, for easy handling, my preference is a pan.

Serve with some boiled rice, a cucumber salad on the side and, of course, a bowl of kimchee.

The meat needs to be well marinated, and the flavour is rich. This recipe uses pear, which lightens the marinade flavours, improving it enormously, in my opinion. You can use either a green eating pear or a nashi (a cross between a pear and apple).

500 g (1 lb) good-quality grilling beef	1 tbsp sugar
½ a firm pear, peeled and cored	¼ tsp black pepper
3 garlic cloves, chopped small	2 tbsp toasted sesame seeds
2 tsp grated fresh ginger	¼ cup (2 fl oz) water
¼ cup (2 fl oz) soy sauce	2 tsp sesame oil

Trim any fat from the meat. It is easier to cut if it's almost frozen. Leave in the freezer for about 30 minutes. Cut into very thin slices, and then cut these so they are approximately 7.5 cm x 5 cm (3 in. x 2 in.). Use your common sense, and if the cut of meat you have bought is not of a shape where these sizes are sensible, trim into approximate slices to suit.

Chop the pear into rough pieces and put into the blender with the garlic, ginger, soy, sugar and pepper, and grind finely.

Crush the sesame seeds with a pestle and mortar or the base of a rolling pin, and add with water and sesame oil. Put the meat into the marinade and stir gently. Leave to marinate for about 3 hours. It can be left longer if you wish, but no more than 8 hours, or the flavours are not as good.

Brush a pan with a little oil and heat. Pick up the meat pieces and shake lightly to drain slightly. Add to the pan, just a few at a time. They must fry quickly, not stew, so keep the heat high. Cook until the meat has changed colour on one side, then turn over and cook just a few seconds on the second side.

Serve immediately, either with or without the dipping sauce.

Serves 4

DIP FOR BULGOGI

This is the traditional dip served with the marinated meat, although I find the flavour of the meat so intense that I am just as happy to eat it plain. It can also be used as a sauce or dip to accompany Western-style grilled chops and steaks.

1 tsp sugar	4 finely-chopped spring onions
1 tbsp rice wine	½ tsp chili sauce
¼ cup (2fl oz) light soy sauce	1 small clove crushed garlic
2 tbsp water	2 tsp toasted sesame seeds

Mix all the ingredients, except for the sesame seeds, together in a bowl. Grind the sesame seeds finely, and add. Stir well and leave at room temperature, if using that day. Otherwise cover tightly and store, refrigerated.

TO SERVE

This dish can be served several ways. You can arrange the meat on a platter with accompaniments on the table, or else you can put a bowl of lettuce in the centre. (Use a soft-leafed lettuce rather than a crisp one.) The meat can be wrapped inside this along with a small spoonful of rice, then the parcel is dipped into the sauce.   Serves 4

GRILLED SPICY FISH

Any small fresh fish (for instance baby bream, snapper) can be used for this dish. Be sure to buy them whole, complete with heads and bones, as this adds to the sweetness of the dish.

6 small whole fish, cleaned	*1 clove crushed garlic*
2 tbsp sesame seeds, toasted	*1 tsp grated ginger*
2 tbsp soy sauce	*¼ tsp chili sauce*
2 tsp sugar	*a little oil*
2 tsp sesame oil	

Grind the sesame seeds and mix all the ingredients (except for the oil) in a shallow bowl. The oil is used to lightly grease a tray which will fit under the griller.

Put the fish, one at a time, into the mixture, turning them so the skin is lightly coated with the sauce. Then transfer to the oiled tray. Put under a very hot griller and cook first on one side, until just flaking, then carefully turn fish over and cook on the other side. Be careful not to overcook.

Serve immediately with any of the juices which come away from the fish. This dish needs only a little rice on the side as accompaniment.

Serves 6

BEAN PANCAKES

These are rather more like a small round patty than a true pancake, and are usually served as an appetiser. They are made with mung beans, peeled and split into halves.

If you are unable to get these beans, chick peas can be substituted. I always use chick peas. The flavour is excellent, but the texture is slightly starchy. They can be served plain or with a dip of chili, soy sauce or some kimchee. I think they need one of these to give them a little 'bite'.

---

1 cup mung beans or chick peas

125 g (4 oz) lean pork, finely minced

1 large egg

2 chopped spring onions (include the green part)

2 cloves crushed garlic

1 tsp salt

½ tsp black ground pepper

1 cup chopped kimchee or

2 large cabbage leaves, very finely shredded and then chopped

1 tsp chili paste

vegetable oil

sesame oil

Put the mung beans or chick peas into a basin. Cover with plenty of water. They will swell and absorb it. Leave to stand for about 12 hours. Drain but retain one cup of the water.

Process them to a purée with this cup of water, and put the mixture into a basin. Add the pork and mash it well into the beans along with the egg, spring onion, garlic, salt, pepper and kimchee or cabbage, and chili. You can prepare the mixture and let it stand for 12 hours if you wish. Be sure to cover well in the refrigerator.

Mix about 1 tablespoon of oil with a teaspoon of sesame oil and brush this over the base of a non-stick frying pan. When the pan is very hot, add a big spoonful of the bean and pork mixture and cook until it is brown underneath, and small bubbles appear. Turn over and cook on the other side. Be sure the pork is cooked through and, if the pan becomes dry at any stage, moisten again with the oil.

As the patties are done, put them into a cloth and cover loosely so they keep warm. They can also be served cold, but are best hot or warm.

Serves 4

CUCUMBER SALAD

This is served on the table with other dishes as an accompaniment. It is only slightly spicy, as I have adjusted the chili. However, you can of course, add more or less of this to suit your own taste.

1 long continental cucumber or	1 tsp sugar
2 short cucumbers	1 tbsp rice wine vinegar
2 tsp salt	1 tsp sesame oil
¾ cup (6 fl oz) water	1 small chili (minus seeds), finely
1 clove crushed garlic	chopped
2 or 3 spring onions, finely sliced	or generous pinch of chili powder

Peel the cucumber and cut into wafer-thin slices, and place in a bowl. Mix in the salt and water and stir well. Stand for about 30 minutes, and then drain thoroughly. Return to the bowl, and chill for several hours.

Mix all the remaining ingredients and, just before serving, add the cucumber. Stir to coat in the mixture. It is served chilled.

If you have some of the salad left over, you can cover it and store in the refrigerator for a day. It will become soft and have more liquid, but will still taste very pleasant.

Serves 4

PHILIPPINES

I was given a small cheap — but according to locals — 'authentic' cookbook when I was in the Philippines. The first page I glanced at made me shudder in horror. 'Saute garlic, onion and tomato' it said. 'Add live frogs, which you have first skinned, and cook them for five minutes or until they can no longer jump up and down in the pan'. In a recipe a few pages on were directions for marinating a chicken in a cup of 7 UP. I mention this to illustrate the strange mixture in Filipino cuisine. The traditional has been strongly influenced by occupying nations.

They have retained their early Chinese-Malay dishes, but you find others, such as a paella of seafood and chicken, with the distinctively Spanish ingredients of olive oil, garlic, onions and red peppers. Later during the war years, judging by their recipes, they appear to have become enchanted with such American ingredients as tomato sauce, mayonnaise, evaporated milk and soft drinks.

However, rice — along with pork and fish — has remained the staple. Rice is eaten at every meal, and between breakfast, lunch and dinner they nibble on a whole range of snacks from ground rice cakes to noodle dishes, tiny pies or sweet pastries.

Little shops offer myriad colourful sweets and ice creams — the Filipinos are renowned for their sweet tooth.

The food of this country, because of the lack of heavy spice and heat found in that of neighbouring countries, is more suitable for serving with wines.

ADOBO

In this dish, the meat is marinated in vinegar. This both tenderises the meat and gives the dish an interesting tart flavour. One of the most popular dishes, adobo is not just a single recipe, it's more a style of cooking. You will find chicken, fish or crab adobo, although the most popular one of all is this one — made with pork. This is almost the national dish. Pepper, garlic and vinegar are the constant ingredients.

Filipinos use palm vinegar which is quite mild and can be bought in many Asian food stores. If you can't obtain it, use a white wine vinegar but dilute with an additional third of a cup of water, as it is much stronger than palm vinegar.

---

*1 kg (2 lb) pork, i.e., pork fillet, or
  a piece of shoulder or leg*
4 cloves garlic, finely chopped
plenty of black ground pepper
3 tbsp soy sauce
½ cup (4 fl oz) palm vinegar

1 bay leaf
1 tbsp oil
*an additional 4 cloves garlic, finely
  chopped*
¾ cup (6 fl oz) water

Cut the meat into large, bite-sized pieces. Allow for removal of fat, making sure you end up with 1 kg of lean pork. Mix the garlic, pepper, soy and vinegar with bay leaf in a bowl. Add pork, stir to coat and leave to marinate about 2 hours.

Heat the oil in a saucepan. Add the additional garlic and cook a minute, stirring until pale golden. Add the meat, marinade and water. Bring to the boil and turn the heat down very low. Let simmer about 1 hour or until the meat is quite tender.

Remove the meat with a slotted spoon and boil down the sauce to give it more flavour. Return the meat and keep warm, or leave to cook. Store refrigerated and reheat gently.

Serves 4

FRESH LUMPIA

This particular dish can either be served fresh, or the thin crepes can be fried in very hot oil after the filling has been rolled inside, rather like a spring roll.

There are a number of versions of this. Some include ground pork and others, chicken and bamboo shoots or fish. One exotic version features the rare heart of the coconut palm.

As this book features healthy food, I have given the recipe for fresh lumpia, a delectable dish which uses a mixture of chicken, pork and prawns with vegetables, although you could vary it as you wish.

OUTSIDE WRAPPERS

4 large eggs   *1 cup flour*

1¼ cups (10 fl oz) water   *2 tbsp oil*

pinch salt

Put the first three ingredients into a food processor or basin and mix for a few seconds. Add flour and mix or beat for a few more seconds. Stir in oil. Let stand, covered for about 20 minutes.

Brush a small crepe or frying pan, 15 cm (6 in.) in diameter, with oil. Heat and add just enough batter to coat the base. If you've added too much, tip out any excess. The first one is usually the worst, until you get into the swing of it. When one side is golden, turn over and cook just a couple of seconds on the other side.

Continue until they are all cooked. They should be pale, not brown, or they will be too crisp. Put them onto a plate on top of each other, as you make them. Cover when they are all finished, but leave at room temperature. They can be prepared about 6 hours in advance.

FILLING

1 tbsp oil	2 carrots, peeled and cut into small
1 onion, finely diced	matchstick pieces
1 clove garlic, finely chopped	2 cups cabbage, finely shredded
½ cup raw green prawns (shrimp),	125 g (4 oz) baby green beans, ends
very finely chopped	removed and beans cut into
¼ cup ham, finely diced	2.5 cm (1 in.) lengths
1 cup cooked chicken breast, cut	½ cup spring onions, finely sliced
into small pieces	some black pepper
1 cup bean shoots, washed	1 tbsp soy sauce

Heat the oil in a large frying pan, add the onion and garlic, and cook until softened. Add the prawns and stir until they have changed colour on the outside. Mix in ham, chicken and all the remaining ingredients, except for spring onions, pepper and soy sauce.

Fry a minute until all the vegetables are hot, then add two tablespoons of water and keep cooking over high heat until barely tender. This should only take a minute. Mix in spring onions, some pepper and soy sauce.

Leave aside at room temperature, but don't keep longer than a couple of hours. If moisture accumulates around the vegetables, drain them lightly before using in the wrappers.

TO ASSEMBLE

Don't assemble until a couple of hours in advance. The filling can be wrapped plain, or with a leaf of cos lettuce (which has been washed and then dried) placed on the wrapper first. Put a wrapper on the bench, then place the lettuce leaf on it, so it protrudes slightly at one end, and add a couple of spoonfuls of the filling.

INDONESIA   Bean Curd Omelette, p.139, is served here with carrot relish, p.140, and rice.

Roll over, so the filling is enclosed. Keep them covered with a piece of plastic wrap. Serve at room temperature with the dipping sauce.

For a party you could put out the piles of egg wrappers on one platter, the filling on another and let people make their own.

TO SERVE

2 tbsp sugar

1 tbsp cornflour (cornstarch)

2 tbsp soy sauce

1 cup (8 fl oz) chicken stock

1 large clove garlic, crushed

Mix all the ingredients, except the garlic, in a saucepan. Heat, stirring constantly until thickened. Add garlic and keep warm, or gently reheat.

Serves 6

RICE WITH CHICKEN

1 chicken, about 1.5 kg (3 lb)	*1 large onion, diced small*
1 tbsp olive oil	*1½ cups rice*
10–12 cloves garlic	*3 cups (24 fl oz) water*
1 piece fresh ginger, about 2.5 cm	*salt and pepper*
(1 in.) in length, sliced and cut	*6 spring onions, cut into thin slices*
into thin slivers	

Remove the legs from the chicken and cut through at the joints.
Remove the wings, and cut the breast section into three. You should
now have nine portions. (You could simply use nine chicken
drumsticks, which can be easily bought in most poultry shops, but
don't use breast of chicken as it becomes very dry.)

Heat the oil and add garlic. Cook gently, stirring until it has turned
a golden colour. Remove. Put the onion and ginger into the pan and
sauté until the onion has slightly softened. If there is not enough oil
you can add more, or simply add a tablespoon of water.

Add the chicken, turn up the heat and cook the chicken pieces until
they have changed colour on the outside. Push to one side, or remove
if the pan is a smallish one.

Add rice and cook a minute, stirring, then mix in half of the garlic,
return chicken pieces if you have removed them, and water. Season
with salt and pepper. Bring to the boil and put a lid on top. Turn the
heat down to its lowest, and cook for 20 minutes. Don't lift the lid
during this cooking time.

Remove the rice and chicken to a large platter or else put out on
individual plates. Scatter the top with spring onion and a little of the
reserved cooked garlic as a garnish. Serve immediately.

Serves 4

BURMA

Burma has a mix of foods influenced by the neighbouring countries, Thailand, China and India.

Soup is always served piping hot and so is rice, but apart from these Burmese dishes are always placed on the table at the same time. Consequently, they quickly become cold, and are eaten at room temperature or luke-warm. Curries are popular, and condiments are pungent, forming an important part of the meal.

Rice is fluffy, long grain rice being the only type used in Burma. It is often cooked in exotic ways, with the fragrance of lemon grass, with coconut milk, or with spices or vegetables.

Once it was customary to eat Burmese food with your fingers, but now forks and spoons are used instead. I have listed two soups, nourishing, easy and very flavoursome. Serve these in deep bowls, so they will retain their heat. You could make a meal of them, together with the rice dish in this section, or you could use the soups as a first course, before any main dish.

SHRIMP RELISH

This is the most popular of all the Burmese accompaniments, a pungent preparation which is eaten with rice and noodles, salads and vegetables or cooked meat. It is invariably served on the table in the same way in which soy sauce appears on a Chinese table.

Store in a sealed jar in the refrigerator. It will keep for weeks.

More oil is used in this than in the other recipes in this book, because it is difficult to make without frying the ingredients, to bring up the flavours.

½ cup (4 fl oz) oil	1 tsp chili powder
10 cloves garlic, sliced	1 tsp salt
1 onion, finely diced	1 tbsp shrimp paste
125 g (4 oz) prawn powder, or	1 tsp turmeric
small dried shrimps	1 tbsp vinegar

Heat oil and fry the garlic over a low heat until golden. Remove immediately with a slotted spoon, and drain on kitchen paper. It will darken as it cools.

Add the onion to the pan and fry this too until golden. Drain and leave to crisp.

If using whole dried shrimp, put these into a food processor and grind until reduced to minute strands.

Add the shrimp powder or puréed dried shrimps to the hot oil with the chili powder, salt, shrimp paste and turmeric, and cook until aromatic. Mix in the vinegar and fry until a thick mixture. Remove and allow to cool, mix in fried onion and garlic, stirring to distribute.

MILD, CLEAR SOUP WITH PRAWNS

This soup has a very good flavour, even when made with a base of water. The ingredients and taste are typically Burmese, and the vegetables can be varied according to what you have on hand. For example, pumpkin, cauliflower, cabbage, marrow or zucchini are all suitable, as long as you have a good proportion of fresh greens.

5 cups water	*1 large onion, finely diced*
45 g (1 ½ oz) shrimp powder or dried shrimp	*185 g (6 oz) pumpkin, cut into very small dice*
2 large cloves garlic, crushed	*1 cup cucumber, (about ½ a cucumber) seeds removed and diced small*
1 tbsp soy	
1 tbsp fish sauce	
¼ tsp black pepper	*½ bunch spinach*

Put the water into a saucepan and add the shrimp powder. If using dried shrimp, process these until ground. Add the garlic, soy, fish sauce, pepper with onion, pumpkin and cucumber. Cook gently, covered, for about 8 minutes, or until tender.

Wash the spinach well, and remove any very tough stalks. Shred the leaves finely. Add to the soup and cook for only a minute or two; the spinach must remain bright green. You need a big cup or ladle to serve this soup, so you can distribute a generous helping of all the vegetables to each person. This soup smells fishy while cooking but, although very tasty, the flavour is more delicate than the aroma indicates.

Serves 6

MILD SOUP WITH CELLOPHANE NOODLES

These clear noodles are not easy to measure but they usually come in tiny bundles, in packets. Use one of these bundles for this soup. If they are not ready-bundled, just take a small handful. The soup is very tasty and easy to prepare. It can be reheated if you wish to make it in advance, but be careful not to overcook the prawns.

1 small bundle cellophane noodles	*125 g (4 oz) raw, shelled prawns*
3 Chinese mushrooms	*1 medium-sized zucchini, cut into*
4 cups (32 fl oz) chicken stock	*small neat dice*
1 onion, halved and thinly sliced	*2 tbsp finely chopped spring onion,*
1 large clove crushed garlic	*including the green tops*
1 tbsp soy	*2 tsp lemon juice*

Put the noodles into a bowl with hot water and let soak until soft. Cut into shorter pieces.

Soak the mushrooms in warm water for about 20 minutes. Remove the stalks and slice the caps thinly.

Bring the chicken stock to the boil in a saucepan, and add onion and garlic. Cook gently for 10 minutes.

Add the mushrooms, soy, prawns and zucchini, and cook another couple of minutes until the prawns and zucchini are cooked.

Check seasoning, add spring onion and lemon just before serving.

Serves 4

BURMESE RICE

Long grain rice is always used in Burma, and served at every meal. In this particular dish, cooked by the absorption method (resulting in tender, plump grains of rice), lemon grass is added to give a delicate citrus taste and aroma.

1½ cups long grain rice	*1 tbsp dried shrimp, soaked for*
1 stalk lemon grass	*20 minutes*
3 cups (24 fl oz) water	*1 tbsp oil*
1 tsp salt	*1 tbsp fish sauce*
1 onion, roughly chopped	*1 tbsp lemon juice*
2 cloves garlic	*1 onion, cut into very thin slices*
1 small chili, seeds removed and	*1 additional tbsp oil*
flesh finely diced	

Put the rice into a heavy-based saucepan. Bang the lemon grass with a heavy knife or meat mallet to bruise it, and push it down into the rice. Add water and bring to the boil. Season with salt, and cover. Simmer very gently for 20 minutes. The rice should now be tender.

Put the roughly-chopped onion, garlic, chili and drained shrimp into a food processor and purée. Heat the oil and fry the mixture until aromatic. Add the fish sauce and lemon.

Heat the remaining oil in a frying pan, add the sliced onion, and cook until it is lightly browned.

When the rice is tender, add the onion, garlic, chili and shrimp mixture, forking it gently through the rice. Cover again and remove from the heat, leaving it to mellow for 5 minutes.

Spoon out into a bowl and scatter the top with the lightly-browned onion.

Serves 4

INDONESIA

Indonesian food contains a wealth of spices; haunting and heady aromas of chili, lemon grass, nutmeg, ginger and galangal scent the air. Herbs and spices are grown in abundance in Indonesia.

Dishes chosen should create a balance on the palate: crunchy cucumber to cool the fire of chili, and mild rice to accompany a sour, tart dish.

Except for soup, which is served hot, food placed on the table is shared and quickly becomes cool, so Indonesian food is always eaten at room temperature. It is picked up with the right hand, and bowls are passed around with the left hand.

Meals are accompanied by very sweet tea or ginger wine.

LAMB SATE

Lamb is very popular in Indonesia. It is usually well-laced with garlic, and the meat itself quite strong. This lamb saté can be barbecued or cooked under a griller (broiler). Instead of the more familiar delicious, but rich, peanut sauce, this is an alternative Indonesian saté sauce with quite an intense flavour. Serve with rice and a variety of vegetables or salad.

1 kg (2 lb) portion leg of lamb	*2 tbsp dark soy sauce*
1 large clove garlic, crushed	*½ tsp ground ginger*
good pinch chili powder	*1 tbsp white wine vinegar (or*
1 tsp ground coriander	*tamarind water)*
2 tbsp finely chopped onion	*1 tbsp oil*

Trim all the fat from the lamb. Cut into pieces of about 3.5 cm (1½ in.) square, so they are bite-sized. Mix all the remaining ingredients in a bowl and add the meat. Stir to coat and leave to marinate, covered and refrigerated, for about 12 hours.

Thread onto soaked bamboo skewers. Cook over charcoal or put under a pre-heated griller, turning them over several times until brown on the outside, but still slightly pink inside.

SAUCE

3 tbsp finely chopped onion	*¼ tsp finely-chopped red or green*
2 tbsp soy sauce	*chili (minus seeds)*
1 tsp sugar	*1½ tbsp lemon juice*

Mix all the sauce ingredients. When the lamb is cooked trickle a little over the top of each skewer while still hot, before serving.

Serves 6

INDONESIAN CHICKEN SOUP

This substantial soup can be eaten before a meal, but it can also be used as a main course, with perhaps just a rice dish or salad to follow.

250 g (8 oz) chicken breast,
   skinned

125 g (4 oz) shelled prawns
   (shrimp)

5 candlenuts

¼ tsp chili powder

1 tsp grated ginger

2 cloves garlic

2 tbsp oil

½ tsp turmeric

4 cups chicken stock

1 tbsp soy sauce

6 young celery leaves, finely
   chopped

1 small handful vermicelli, broken
   into small pieces

1 cup bean sprouts

Cut the chicken into small dice. Cut the prawns into halves or smaller, depending on their size. Put the candlenuts, chili powder, ginger and garlic into a food processor and purée.

Heat the oil in a large saucepan, and add the paste. Fry until aromatic, and add the chicken. Cook, stirring, until it has changed colour, and mix in the turmeric and prawns.

Fry for a minute, then pour over half the stock, and cover, simmering gently for 2 minutes. Add the remainder of the stock and soy, and the celery leaves and vermicelli, and cook until the vermicelli is almost tender, adding bean shoots for the last 30 seconds. Taste and adjust the seasonings.

You can serve this with lemon pieces, and scatter with spring onion if you wish.

Serves 4 as soup
Serves 2 as main course

INDONESIAN-STYLE GRILLED FISH

In this dish, a rather strong but immensely tasty topping on the fish flavours the skin and creates a light coating. If you don't want too hot a dish, you can cut down the chili, but leave in just a little for the right balance of flavours.

Any small fish can be used for this dish. Allow one per person, and have them cleaned and scaled but leave on the bone, for the sweetest flavour. The coating mixture can be prepared about 12 hours in advance, but refrigerate it and be sure to cover well so it doesn't permeate all the food.

---

4 small whole fish, e.g bream, baby snapper, mullet

1 medium-sized onion, chopped very roughly

1 small chili (minus seeds), chopped

6 candlenuts

3 tsp sugar

2 medium-sized tomatoes, roughly chopped

¼ tsp laos powder

½ tsp salt

1 tbsp oil

Rinse the fish and pat dry. Put onion, chili, candlenuts, sugar, tomato into a food processor or blender, and process until a coarse mixture. Add the laos powder and salt.

Put the fish on a lightly oiled sheet of non-stick baking paper and spread the mixture over the top, patting down to make a coating.

Bake in a moderate oven (190°C/350°F–400°F), for about 12–15 minutes, or until fish just flakes when touched with a knife. Timing will depend on thickness, but be careful not to overcook.

Carefully lift from the paper, and serve immediately with salad and rice.

Serves 4

BEAN CURD OMELETTE

A very high-protein dish, the soft bean curd makes a slightly granular-looking mixture when you pour it into the pan, but once cooked this omelette will be quite smooth on the outside, and is very silky to eat. Don't overcook the top part. Roll it over while slightly wet and let it sit for about 30 seconds. It will continue cooking, and be soft and tender.

200 g (13 oz) bean curd, (tofu)	*1 little white pepper*
4 eggs	*generous pinch cayenne or few*
1 tsp salt	*drops chili oil or minced chili*
¼ cup finely-chopped spring onion	*1 tbsp oil*

Put the bean curd in a small bowl and mash with a fork. Beat the eggs with remaining ingredients, except for the oil, and when well mixed stir in the mashed bean curd.

Brush the base of a non-stick omelette pan with oil. When hot tip in half the mixture, tilting the pan so it is thinly covered. Cook over a moderate heat until the base is golden and set.

Fold the two sides into the centre and let it cook gently in the pan for another 30 seconds. The outside heat of the egg will gently set the centre.

Turn out onto a plate and add a little more oil to make the second omelette in the same manner. (Or you can make one large omelette, and cut into halves.)

Serve with rice, carrot relish and a little soya sauce.

Serves 2

CARROT RELISH

4 small young carrots (about
   200 g/13 oz)
1 tsp salt

1 tbsp white wine vinegar
1 tbsp brown sugar

Peel the carrots and cut into very fine shreds, like little matchsticks. Put salt, white wine vinegar and sugar into a bowl. Add carrots and work with your fingers, so carrots are well covered. Leave to stand, refrigerated, for several hours.

Drain well before serving. The carrots will have a crisp texture and lightly pickled taste. A small bundle of these is spooned alongside the omelette. These carrots can also be used as a relish with a rice and meat meal.

Serves 2 generously

EGGPLANT IN A SOY SAUCE

This makes a tasty side dish, or it can be served with rice and a salad for a very light lunch.

3 small eggplant (about 500 g/1 lb
   altogether)
salt
1 tbsp oil
1 large onion, halved, then thinly
   sliced
2 ripe tomatoes, finely diced

1 large clove garlic, crushed
1 tbsp soy sauce
2 tbsp water
2 tsp lemon juice
2 tsp sugar
¼ tsp chili powder

Wash the eggplant, cut into halves and then into wedges, lengthwise.

Scatter with salt, stand 30 minutes, and rinse. Pat dry.

Heat the oil in a frying pan, add the onion and cook gently until slightly softened, stirring occasionally.

Add the garlic and eggplant wedges, cook for about 6 minutes, then turn them over and cook over a low heat for another 2 minutes.

Add tomato and remaining ingredients. Simmer gently about 10 minutes with a lid on the pan. Turn the eggplant over if not cooking evenly.

Serves 6

CARROT STIR-FRY

The Dutch introduced carrots to Indonesia, where they are called 'wortel', which rings strangely in the Indonesian language. This stir-fry could be served as part of an Asian meal, but is also good to accompany a Western meal.

500 g (1 lb) young carrots	*1 large clove crushed garlic*
1 tbsp oil	*½ cup (4 fl oz) chicken stock*
¼ tsp finely-chopped, seeded chili	*2 tsp soy sauce*
2 tbsp finely-chopped shallots	*1 tsp sugar*

Peel the carrots and cut them into slices lengthwise and then into halves and across, to form small neat matchstick strips.

Heat the oil in a saucepan, add the chili and shallots, and stir for 30 seconds. Mix in the garlic and carrots and cook, stirring for a minute.

Pour in the stock and soy sauce. Add the sugar and bring to the boil. Cover and cook gently for about 3 minutes, or until barely tender. Remove the lid and boil until the liquid has reduced around the carrots.

Serves 4

SIMPLE NASI GORENG

Nasi Goreng, the Indonesian version of fried rice, is a great favourite and has numerous variations. It makes a meal in itself when it is served with such traditional accompaniments as lettuce, sliced tomato and thin slices of cucumber.

It is usually served on a large platter with lettuce at the ends, and the slices of tomato and cucumber on top. If you wish you can place a platter of prawn crackers on the table.

The most important thing of all is to have the rice for the base cooked at least 12 hours in advance, so it is cold and has dried slightly.

---

3 eggs

1 tbsp water

5 cups cold steamed rice

2 small chili (minus seeds) cut into pieces

3 tbsp warm water

2 tbsp oil

185 g (6 oz) shelled green prawns (jumbo shrimp), cut into quarters

125 g (4 oz) chicken breast, skinned and diced small

5 finely-diced spring onions

2 tbsp soy sauce

2 tsp sugar

a little pepper

lettuce, cucumber, tomatoes (for garnish)

Beat the eggs with water. Make 4 thin omelettes, one after another, in a non-stick pan, or use a little oil to grease the base. Let them cook gently rather than over a high heat, so the egg sets well. Turn each one out onto a board and let cool. Roll over and cut into strips.

Put the chili and water into a blender, and purée.

Heat oil in a large frying pan or wok, and add the chili. Cook until the water has evaporated. Add prawns and chicken, and toss for a

couple of minutes. Then add spring onions and rice, and mix the rice with the prawns and chicken.

Finally, add the soy, sugar and pepper. Mix together and toss for a couple of minutes until everything is heated and the rice coated lightly with soy. Spoon out onto a warmed platter and scatter the egg shreds on top, then the garnish.

Serves 4

DESSERTS   Light and refreshing Fruit Salad with Mango Sauce, p.152, Pineapple in Aromatic Sauce, p.153 and Indian Rice Pudding, p.154.

145

SRI LANKA

'Add half a cup of coconut milk' . . . 'Pour in two cups of coconut milk'. A major component of many of my favourite Sri Lankan dishes, coconut milk is high in saturated fat, an ingredient which should be omitted from low-fat diets. For this reason this chapter is tiny — just a small glimpse of the wonderful diversity of dishes from the beautiful island poetically called 'the pearl in the ear of India'.

Curries are of major importance here, with sauces generously mingling with coconut in most cases, and rice served with most meals, even when bread is included.

The meal is always accompanied by sambals, freshly made each day, and everything is placed on the table at the same time — with little regard for keeping it hot. Dishes should, however, always be chosen to complement each other.

This small selection could be served at one meal. But it would be better to use either the fish accompanied by rice and the bean shoot sambal, or the Jaggery Satay with the sambal and rice.

SPICY BARBECUED FISH

This dish is meant to be barbecued, wrapped in banana leaves, but these aren't always available, unless you live in a warm climate. It can be successfully cooked wrapped in foil, although this takes a little longer and, of course, picks up none of the flavours of the leaf. Nevertheless, it is still delicious cooked in foil, and is an ideal dish for a barbecue.

4 small fish, eg bream, baby snapper or mullet	2 slices fresh ginger
2 tbsp lemon juice	¼ tsp cinnamon
1 tsp turmeric	1 tsp ground cumin
½ tsp salt	1 tbsp ground coriander
¼ tsp ground black pepper	¼ tsp cloves ground
1 large onion, roughly chopped	¼ tsp chili oil or 1 small chili
2 cloves garlic	1 tbsp oil

Leave the fish whole, but clean, scale and rinse it. Pat dry. Cut several diagonal slashes in the thickest part, near the head. Rub with lemon juice. Mix turmeric with salt and pepper and scatter on top, then rub in.

Put the onion with garlic, ginger and remaining ingredients into a food processor until a fine mixture. Have 4 pieces of foil, larger than the fish, and oil lightly.

Put a little of the mixture on one side of the fish, turn quickly over onto the foil and divide the remainder of the mixture over the top. Rub well into the slashes of the fish. Fold over the foil, sealing well, and tuck up the ends so you have a firm package.

If cooking over a barbecue, the timing will depend on the heat and thickness of the fish. If grilling, preheat the griller (broiler) first, and put the packages on a flat baking tray. Timing can vary considerably — you will need to check the packages — but give them approximately 10 minutes each side.

They can also be cooked in the oven. Again, place them on a flat tray and allow about 20 minutes in a moderate oven 190°C (350°F-400°F).

To serve, unwrap a little from the top, but leave the packages on the plates, so you have the full effect of all the aroma and juices.

Serves 4

BEAN SPROUT SAMBAL

All kinds of interesting sambals, relishes and pickles are served with Sri Lankan food. I have chosen this one, which can accompany rice or any of the meat or fish dishes, because it is so fresh tasting and bean shoots are so healthy. It is best if made at least an hour before eating to allow the flavour of the spices to enhance the bean shoots.

3 cups bean sprouts	*1 small chili (minus seeds), finely*
3 tbsp desiccated coconut	*diced*
1 small onion, very finely diced	*½ tsp salt*
1 tbsp lemon juice	

Rinse the bean shoots and drain well.

Put the coconut into a bowl, cover with boiling water and let stand for about 10 minutes. Drain. Mix with the onion, lemon, chili and salt. Add to the bean shoots and stir very well to mix. The coconut tends to stay in a lump at first, so you need to spend a few minutes mixing. Cover and chill.

Serves 4 as an accompaniment

JAGGERY SATAY

Jaggery is palm sugar, obtainable in some Asian shops, with an intense caramel flavour. If you can't buy it, dark brown sugar makes an acceptable substitute. This is a sweet and sour dish, and should be served with rice. It can be prepared well in advance as it reheats well.

500 g (1 lb) lean casserole beef, eg	*1 tsp chili paste*
chuck or blade steak	*¼ tsp salt and black pepper*
1 ½ tbsp tamarind	*2 tbsp jaggery or dark brown sugar*
¾ cup (6 fl oz) hot water	*1 tbsp oil*

Cut the beef into pieces of about 2.5 cm (1 in) in size. Put the tamarind into a bowl, pour on the ¾ cup of hot water, and soak for 10 minutes. Squeeze with your fingers and then strain. Mix into this the remaining ingredients, except for the oil.

Heat the oil in a saucepan, add the meat, a little at a time, and stir until it has changed colour, removing each batch and then adding more. When it has all been coloured, return to the pot with the tamarind mixture and bring slowly to the boil.

Cover and simmer over a low heat until the meat is tender, about 1½–1¾ hours. Taste and season with more salt and pepper, if you wish.

Serves 4

DESSERTS

Even the most dedicated devotees of Asian food will admit that few Asian desserts appeal to Western palates. This is partly because we eat them differently, always keeping our sweets for the finish of the meal.

In Asian countries, sweet items are usually eaten as snacks between, rather than after, a meal; platters of fruit, or one piece of perfectly ripe, luscious fruit, being eaten at the end of the meal.

Many of my favourite Asian desserts couldn't be included here. Very sweet, with lots of coconut milk or cream, or fried in batter, they are wonderful but they should be regarded only as an occasional treat.

Instead I have chosen recipes which I think create a light finish for the menus in this book. Some of them do come from countries listed, others are just fancies of my own.

TROPICAL FRUITS WITH A SPICY PALM SUGAR SAUCE

An Indonesian favourite, this dessert is usually prepared with firm, slightly unripe tropical fruit which then has a sweet, hot and freshly acid sauce poured on top. I find it better to use riper fruit because, while tropical fruits may still have plenty of flavour when just picked and sliced for the table in Indonesia, here they are hard and very sharp unless ripe.

It is a lovely dessert. Don't be deterred by the darkness of the sauce made from tamarind — it doesn't look particularly attractive, but has a lovely flavour.

1 tbsp tamarind	*2 oranges*
½ cup (4 fl oz) water	*½ small paw paw (papaya)*
3 slices chili	*1 mango*
½ cup palm sugar or brown sugar	*4 slices fresh pineapple*

Put the tamarind into a bowl, cover with warm water, and let it soak for about 5 minutes. Then work with your fingers to mix, and strain. Discard all the dark, fibrous bits.

Put the tamarind water with the chili and palm sugar into a blender. If the sugar is still slightly granulated it will soften as it stands.

Peel the orange, removing all the white pith, and take out segments. Remove seeds and peel from paw paw, and cut it into thin slices. Peel the mango and cut into slices from the stone.

Put a circle of pineapple in the centre of large plates and arrange the fruits from this in a fan shape. Serve chilled with the sauce in a separate jug.

Serves 4

FRUIT SALAD WITH MANGO SAUCE

Although you can vary the fruit, don't use too many or you get no particular flavour. It is also best to cut the fruit into pieces large enough to retain their character. Eat this the day it is made, although the mango sauce can be prepared 24 hours in advance (if refrigerated and well covered).

1 small paw paw (papaya) or half a large one	*1 mango or 1 can (450 g/1 lb) tinned mango*
1 punnet (250 g/8 oz) strawberries	*½ cup (4 fl oz) orange juice*
2 kiwi fruit	*1 tbsp castor sugar*
1 cup fresh pineapple pieces	

Remove seeds from the paw paw, peel and cut into bite-sized pieces. Hull the berries. If very large, they can be halved. Peel the kiwi fruit and cut into thick slices. Put all the fruit into a bowl.

Peel the fresh mango, cut the flesh away from the stone and purée it. If you're using canned mango, drain the juice from it and purée the mango slices in the tin.

Mix the mango pulp with orange juice and sugar and stir so the sugar will soften. If too thick, add a little more orange juice. Put about a third of a cup of this over the fruit and mix very gently. Chill the fruit and mango sauce.

At dinnertime, put the fruit in individual dessert dishes or wine glasses and spoon over more of the mango sauce. You can decorate with a sprig of mint or tiny flower if you wish.

Serves 6

PINEAPPLE IN AN AROMATIC SAUCE

This dessert improves if you can leave it to marinate for about 12 hours. The flavours of the spices are elusive but give a beautiful fragrance to the pineapple. Serve it chilled, and plain. Ice cream or cream are quite unnecessary.

½ cup (4 fl oz) water	6 cardamon pods
2 tbsp sugar	12 slices fresh pineapple
1 cinnamon stick	¼ cup shelled and skinned
12 coriander seeds	pistachio nuts

Heat the water and sugar. Add the cinnamon stick. Crush the coriander seeds and cardamon pods with the end of a rolling pin or in a pestle and mortar. Mix into the water and sugar and bring slowly to the boil. Turn off the heat and leave it to steep for about 30 minutes.

Put the pineapple into a bowl, pour the syrup through a sieve over the top. Cover and chill at least 4 hours before serving.

Arrange the pineapple in a shallow dish with a raised rim, so you can spoon over the syrup. Cut the pistachio nuts into halves and scatter on top.

Serves 6

INDIAN RICE PUDDING

Smooth and creamy, flavoured with cardamon and rose water, this pudding is usually made with a rich milk, but is still lovely with skim milk. Eat it plain or with fresh or poached fruits. You can serve it warm or chilled, but if refrigerating cover it so it won't get a skin on top.

¾ (6 fl oz) cup skim milk	2 tbsp sugar
2 tbsp ground rice	½ tsp ground cardamon
1 cup (8 fl oz) additional skim milk	1 tsp rose water

Mix the skim milk with ground rice in a basin and stir well to mix.

Heat the additional milk with sugar and when just beginning to bubble on the edges, tip into the bowl of milk and ground rice, stirring.

Return to the saucepan and stir constantly until it comes to the boil and lightly thickens. Leave to cook over the lowest heat for a couple of minutes.

Remove, and mix in the cardamon and rose water. Pour into individual dessert dishes or wine glasses and let cool slightly. It will thicken more as it stands.

NOTE: It is best to use a non-stick saucepan, if you have one, because this mixture sticks to the base and burns quickly if not watched carefully.

Serves 4 (tiny serves)

A THAI-STYLE BANANA DISH

Very fresh-tasting, this quickly cooked dish of sautéed bananas with lemon and lime juice was once given to me as a Thai dessert, although I must admit I'm not sure if it's authentic.

4 bananas

30 g (1 oz) butter

4 tbsp brown sugar

1 tbsp lemon juice

juice 2 small limes

Peel bananas and cut each into two, lengthwise.

Melt the butter and, when foaming, add bananas. Turn the heat down and cook very gently, turning them once, until almost softened.

Add sugar, and cook gently a minute longer until there is a little syrup in the pan. Squeeze lemon on top and shake the pan.

Put several banana pieces on each serving plate. Squeeze the juice of a half a lime over each one, and serve immediately. Serves 4

KHEER

This is an Indian dish, eaten on religious and special occasions.

½ cup rice

6 cups skim milk

4 cardamon pods

¾ cup sugar

3 tbsp slivered blanched almonds

2 tbsp sultanas

½ tsp rose water

some ground cardamon or nutmeg

for the top of the dessert

Wash the rice well, and cook for 5 minutes in a generous amount of water. Drain. Heat the skim milk with cardamon pods. When bubbling on the edges, add the rice and cook on the lowest heat until the rice is quite soft. It will take about 45 minutes. Stir frequently, then add the sugar, almonds and sultanas. Mix them through gently.

Cool slightly, and stir through rose water. Remove the cardamon pods and pour the dessert into small, individual dishes. Leave to cool. Scatter the top with a little ground cardamon or nutmeg and serve at room temperature. Serves 6

SPECIAL INGREDIENTS

Tips on buying, using and storing them. See also pages 59 and 100, respectively, for Japanese and Indian ingredients.

BASIL
Several varieties of this herb are grown in Thailand, where it is used with abandon as both a flavouring and a vegetable. Any local basil can be used in Thai dishes, except for the 'opal' basil which has a reddish-purple leaf. This is best in cooking rather than served raw as a garnish. The green-leafed basil is best as a garnish.

BEAN CURD
This is often sold as tofu. It has a bland flavour and is prepared from mashed cooked soya beans formed into a cake. There are many types available, but these recipes require the plain soft, almost custard-textured, bean curd. It is a very high source of protein.

BEAN SPROUTS
Sprouted mung beans, sometimes called bean shoots, are sold in supermarkets and Asian shops. They should be white, crisp and plump. Store in the refrigerator in water, to be changed every day. They will keep well for about 4 days. In fine Chinese cooking, the tiny thread-like root is plucked off, but this is a tedious job and not essential. It is more important to do this if the bean sprout ends have dried or are not so fresh.

CANDLENUTS
This nut is an important ingredient in Indonesian cooking. It is not eaten on its own, but when cooked has a nutty flavour and creamy texture. Its name derives from the fact that they are sometimes threaded on to the middle rib of a palm leaf and used as candles, in Indonesia.
    They are usually bought in packets in Asian shops, and are ground in dishes by placing into a food processor or pounding with a pestle and mortar. Macadamia or cashew nuts could be used as a substitute.

CELLOPHANE NOODLES
These are very fine, transparent noodles, sometimes called 'bean thread vermicelli'. They are made from the starch of green mung beans. In Burmese cooking, they are usually taken from the packet and fried, but, for the health conscious, I recommend they are gently boiled until tender. These noodles are so fine that simply soaking them in hot water before use can be enough.

CHILI
These can vary a lot in colour, size, shape and heat. You need to experiment a little, and to err on the side of caution if in doubt. Handle carefully. Cut into halves, wash out the seeds and then slice, making sure you don't touch your eyes or face afterwards, or they will burn. Always wash your hands thoroughly after handling chilies.
    Several chopped chili products, sold in jars, can now be bought in supermarkets and Asian shops. However, make sure they are purely chili and don't include other ingredients which would alter the flavour of the dish.
    Hot cayenne pepper could be used as a substitute. However, it does not have quite the same complexity as chilies, just the heat.
    Store fresh chilies in the refrigerator, wrapped first in kitchen paper and then in loose plastic. If any become soft, discard, or the others will also begin to rot. They should keep for several weeks.
    Chilies are a good source of vitamins C and A, if you eat enough of them.

CHINESE CABBAGE
The type used for kimchee is a long, pale, wide-ribbed cabbage which springs up and tapers away from the base. It can be bought in some greengrocers and in Asian shops. It is surprisingly easy to grow.

CHINESE PARSLEY   See coriander.

CORIANDER
This is a flat-leaf herb, musky in flavour and pungent. It is also called cilentro and Chinese parsley. Add cautiously at first, if you're not sure whether you care for it, or substitute parsley. It is sold in small bunches with the tiny root remaining. This is often ground in dishes as a flavouring. When the leaves are used, pluck these from the stalk.

DRIED MUSHROOMS   See mushrooms.

DRIED SHRIMPS
These tiny preserved shelled shrimps have a strong flavour, so use them sparingly. Soak in warm water for about 30 minutes before using and, once open, store in a sealed container.

FISH SAUCE (Nam Pla)
Made from fish, layered with salt and left to ferment, the liquid extract is filtered and boiled. It has a salty flavour, although it can vary according to the region where it is made. It is strong, so use sparingly. This is as important to Thai and Vietnamese cooking as soy sauce is to Chinese. Once opened, it will keep almost indefinitely in a cool place.

FIVE-SPICE POWDER
A fragrant mix of spices. It usually includes cinnamon, cloves, nutmeg, with variations, such as Sichuan peppercorns, star anise, fennel and licorice root. Mostly for marinades or as a dipping powder. Only a little is needed, as it is quite strong.

HOISIN SAUCE
A sweetish sauce made from fermented beans, or sometimes from pumpkin. Thick in texture, it is mixed into marinades or served as a dipping sauce.

LAOS
A member of the ginger family, this is the spicy root of the 'greater galangal'. Extensively used in Indonesian cooking, you can buy dry pieces of laos and also a powdered form. I have read that the latter is not as good, but is often the only form available. It is very delicate, and I must confess that its flavour is often difficult to detect. This may not be the case with the fresh laos. So if you can't obtain it, you could leave it out without greatly affecting the dish.

LEMON GRASS
This can be bought fresh at markets, and is not difficult to grow at home in any temperate climate. It grows in a clump with long grey-greenish spear-like leaves. These are removed and discarded; only the lower bulbous section is used — the outside tough part of the stalk is taken off, and the inner section is finely chopped. Dried lemon grass can be bought in Asian shops, although this doesn't have much flavour unless it's very fresh. As a substitute you can add a little grated lemon rind.

MUSHROOMS (DRIED)
There are two kinds of Chinese dried mushrooms: black mushrooms and tree-ear mushrooms.
    Black mushrooms: These have a smokey flavour, and fresh mushrooms cannot be substituted. They need to be soaked, the tough stalks removed and caps sliced. Once opened, always store in a cool place in an airtight plastic bag. I have read that a dried red chili in the bag will discourage any bugs.
    Tree-ear mushrooms (cloud ears): These add a crunchy texture and colour, rather than flavour, to dishes. They should be soaked in hot water to soften, and expand.

PALM SUGAR
Sweet, brown and slightly caramel in flavour, it is made from the nectar of the coconut flower, and is available in large blocks or broken pieces. It can usually be bought in Asian shops, but brown sugar can be substituted.

PEANUTS
The peanut garnishes used in Thai cooking have more flavour if the peanuts are roasted. You can buy ready-roasted peanuts in packets. These are quite satisfactory.

PRAWN PASTE (SHRIMP PASTE)
The easiest way to buy this is in jars. It is dark in colour, salty, quite strong-smelling. Only a little is used, and it will blend with ingredients to add pungency. (This is quite different from the dried shrimp paste, sold in blocks.) Although not quite the same, anchovy paste can be substituted.

RED CURRY PASTE
Used in Thai cooking, you can buy it in packets or jars at Asian food stores. It is hot and aromatic, but has an even better flavour if you make your own (see page 13). It keeps about 6 weeks in a glass jar in the refrigerator.

RICE VINEGAR
A mild-flavoured vinegar with a mellow taste. Don't substitute Western-style vinegar, because it is too harsh.

RICE WINE
A yellow grain wine which is used in Asian cooking. The best is known as Shao-hsing, imported from China and Taiwan. If unavailable you can substitute Japanese sake, mirin, a sweetened Japanese cooking wine, dry Vermouth, Scotch or dry sherry.

SESAME OIL
The type used in these recipes is the dark rich oil made from toasted sesame seeds. It has a strong flavour, so use it sparingly.

SESAME SEED PASTE
This is such an important ingredient in Korean cooking that it is a good idea to prepare more than you need for one meal. It can be stored in a screw top-jar in the refrigerator for about a week. Put a cup of white sesame seeds into a dry frying pan. Let them heat, stirring so they colour evenly. When they are golden and smell nutty, remove to bowl. Don't leave in the pan or they continue to cook and may darken too much. Either process in a blender or grind with a pestle and mortar to a coarse ground mixture.

SICHUAN PEPPER
Reddish and brown peppercorns used as a seasoning. Toasted until they smoke and then crushed, they can be mixed with salt as a dipping powder or to add heat to Asian dishes.

SOY SAUCE
The most important ingredient in Chinese cooking, it can vary in saltiness and taste, so you should always taste it. You may need to adjust the seasonings in the recipes accordingly. Buy a good quality soy — it must be naturally fermented and aged. Never buy a chemically-processed one. I used Kikkoman soy (a Japanese brand) for all the recipes in the book.

TAMARIND
Sometimes labelled 'Asam', tamarind is the fruit of the tamarind tree, treasured for the slight acidity it gives to dishes. Indian cooks claim it has digestive properties. It comes in a block, is very dark in colour and you cut off a piece, and soak it in warm to hot water for about 5 minutes. Then squeeze it with your fingers to extract the juice, and pour through a strainer to remove the fibrous matter. Each recipe will give you the exact amounts of tamarind and water.

TURMERIC
Bright yellow in colour, this is the main colouring in curry and is also used to give colour to several dishes, either being mixed into a powder as a spicy topping or to add colour to the skin of fish or meat. It is a rhizome of the ginger family.

VERMICELLI OR CELLOPHANE NOODLES
A dried noodle made from rice flour. You can buy these thick, medium or thin.

WATER CHESTNUTS
Fresh chestnuts are not easy to find, but canned ones are easily bought. Canned chestnuts should be covered with boiling water, drained and then rinsed in fresh water to remove the tinny taste. Stored in cold water in the refrigerator, they will keep for at least one week if the water is changed every day.

INDEX